Arcaro's Interrogation Case Law Book

Author: Gino Arcaro
Website: www.ginoarcaro.com
Email: gino@ginoarcaro.com

Editor: Janice Augustine
Layout & Design: Shelley Palomba

Copyright © Jordan Publications Inc. 2014

Jordan Publications Inc.
Canada

Arcaro, Gino, 1957
ISBN 978-1-927851-09-8
http://www.ginoarcaro.com
Printed in Canada

Volume Series – the breakdown

When I was a rookie detective, my team's staff-sergeant assigned me to put together a book called "Interrogation Case Law of the Week" for the detective office. That was 1984. No internet, no world-wide web, no Google, no Youtube, no social media. I thought it was an initiation. Hazing.

Case law decisions were sent to me. I had to put them into a binder in some sort of logical order. I soon discovered that one binder would not be enough. The Charter was only two years old in 1984. The Confessions Rule was in its never-ending evolution. There was no shortage of decisions.

I had trouble figuring out how to organize the Cases. I tried to make a table of contents. I tried to make chapters. Finally, I asked my partner for advice. "Should I make separate volumes or cram it all into one binder?" He told me not to expect any help from him or anyone else in the detective office, never to ask any questions, and to figure it out on my own. To solve the problem, I simply added new cases at the back of the binder.

Then I was assigned to make an interrogation case law presentation to the entire detective office. Teach the rest of the detectives about new case law, including Charter decisions. Another prank I thought; I was a 26-year-old detective, on a six-month probationary period, in an office full of old-school veteran detectives, many old enough to be my father or grandfather. I thought this was part of the test that I was told about on my first day as a detective: *"If you fuck up once, you're back in uniform."*

My lesson plans for the presentation were a nightmare – a jigsaw puzzle straight out of the box – pieces all over the place. A mess. All the literature I had read up to that point centered on Rules of Evidence – mechanical recitation of Rules of Evidence without the practical application part. Memorize and regurgitate without instruction on how to put in into practice. So I did the same. I just threw one Rule of Evidence after another up on the screen, in no particular order. But I didn't get kicked out of the detective office.

Several years later, I started teaching in college to wannabe-cops straight out of high school without any law enforcement experience as a point of reference. It wasn't until I copied how I taught football – rules first, playbook second – that my lesson plans finally began to take shape. It's the same format I've used for this book series. Because I believe it's impossible to write one book about Canadian interrogation case law, I've divided the series into Volumes.

Volumes one and two explain the basics rules of confession admissibility that have undergone significant change in the 21st century. Subsequent Volumes explain the case law in relation to the interrogation sequence.

<u>Volume One:</u> How the "Contemporary Confessions Rule," from *R. v. Oickle* (2000) applies to confession admissibility.

<u>Volume Two:</u> Focuses on Sec. 24(2) Charter, the landmark case *R. v. Grant* (2009) and the basic case laws that deal with how to prevent Charter violations. Part Two of this volume teaches how to get a "true confession."

<u>Volume Three:</u> The beginning of the "Playbook." Derivative Case Law: Case law decisions that are derived from the Confessions Rule and Charter cases (those that apply interrogation laws).

<u>Volume Four:</u> Case law relating to all the information that an accused person or suspect has to be informed of, including the caution and Charter rights to silence, reason for arrest, and right to counsel.

<u>Volume's Five - Eight:</u> Explanation of "contextual" proper inducement, referring to case law interrogation strategies that have been cleared for use to get a true confession.

Assumptions

The use of the word, "Charter" refers to the Charter of *Rights and Freedoms*, from the *Constitution Act, 1982.*

The term, "Criminal Code" or abbreviation, "C.C." refers to the *Criminal Code R.S.C., 1985, c.C-46.*

CONTENTS

Chapter Zero

CONTINUED

Chapter Zero
It's Easy to Put Down if you Don't Look Up.

Long ago, I renamed 'Preface' in my books to 'Chapter Zero' for one reason – to encourage the audience to read it instead of passing it over. The word 'Preface' had a reputation of being boring. Chapter Zero sounds more interesting. I was hoping to attract more readers to the preface in order to help them decide whether the book was interesting enough to *keep* reading. If Chapter Zero bombs, readers drop it. If it doesn't bomb, they won't be able to put it down. Dual meaning. Readers won't be able to stop reading it and they won't criticize it without reading all of it. If you're going to put something down, you need to build a case. You need strong evidence. The same applies to the topic of interrogation

It's easy to put down if you don't look up. It's always been fashionable to put down the police, the whole concept of interrogation, even the word 'interrogation' itself without looking up – looking up the full extent of confession rules of evidence, including countless case law decisions. But, it's almost impossible to look it all up because of the sheer volume of interrogation case law that keeps growing.

Chapter Zero is the starting point – it sets the tone for this module. This Chapter Zero has 10 Points:

Point #1:   **The beginning and ending of this book are the same.**

Try to carry a heavy burden. You can't. No one can. It will crush you if you don't lift it off. Think of how many times in our lives we've had to get something we've done wrong off our chest to save our soul from extended torture. Think of how difficult it was to hold it inside, to lock up a secret sin. There's an inner force that drives the truth out of us for our own good. Confessing wrongdoing is natural.

Despite what critics want us to believe, confessing the truth is not 'psychological manipulation.' The need to tell *someone* the whole story, or parts of it, is driven by a force of nature – one that applies pressure until the truth leaks out all at once or in small pieces over time. Think of how often it has happened to you – when you've spilled the truth to *someone* and when someone has leaked the truth effortlessly to you, for no apparent reason.

I learned to keep this in mind when an investigation became a heavy burden – the truth will be told to someone. Guaranteed. The key is finding that person or becoming that person. Or both.

Point #2:   **This book boils down to one word – conscience.**

Here's the conclusion of this module: "Make the conscience work." Triple meaning – make it work out, make it work right, make it do all the work. Use your conscience, appeal to the suspect's conscience. That's the simple conclusion that I always focus on because it's too easy to get lost in the sea of interrogation rules of evidence and interrogation case law if you lose focus. This conclusion is a two-way street; i) your conscience is your best guide in the interrogation to get the truth, and, ii) the suspect's conscience makes the interrogation as simple or as complicated as it can get.

Every interrogation is a psychological battle of conscience. No exceptions. Getting a true confession is an exercise that pits conscience versus conscience. When there's a match, the suspect tells you the truth. When there isn't, you won't get the truth. The suspect's conscience is either your partner or your worst enemy. It depends on how strong or weak it is and how strong or weak you can make it.

The conscience is the force of nature that always wins. It always gets its way. It either brings peace by driving the truth or it builds an inner hell until the truth is told. It all depends on the exercise of free will. The connection between the fitness of conscience, free will, and soul is part of the interrogation **intangibles** – the behind-the-scenes work that can't always be seen.

Point #3: **There is no interrogation rulebook or interrogation playbook in the Criminal Code.**

The Criminal Code explains how to search for physical evidence, how to seize physical evidence – breath and blood samples – how to charge an offender, when you can arrest an offender, but there is no "how-to-get-a-true-clean confession," no concrete guidelines for the police to follow, no "interrogation model" in Canadian law that tells you exactly how to get a confession from a suspect. The Charter draws boundaries but gives no strategy. You have to figure it out by studying the interrogation rulebook and playbook that are spread out over Canadian statutes and case law.

It's hard to believe that we're well into the 21st century but there's still no Canadian statute or provision called "Admissibility of Adult Confessions." Confession laws are governed by the Confessions Rule and section 24(2) Charter that only explains the intended outcome – confessions have to be voluntary, reliable, and Charter-violation-free. It's the equivalent of football rulebook that would say, *"touchdowns have to be clean and penalty-free"* while providing no how-to rules to achieve a penalty-free touchdown. The solution is to research case law.

Why is case law important for interrogation? Because that's where interrogation strategy is found. To become an interrogation expert, you have to become a case law expert. Case law answers what-if questions. These answers form an instruction manual. But the problem is volume and mixed messages. Case law is almost infinite. Not all of it is binding law but all of it is persuasive law. And researching it takes time – time that you don't have when you're working in the field or on the frontline.

Point #4: **Nothing just happens.**

I was a police officer for 15 years, from 1975-1990. Nine years uniform branch, six years as a detective. There's nothing I loved more than interrogation. Nothing was a bigger investigative challenge. The pressure, the degree of difficulty, the significance, sense of urgency… it never got boring. I became obsessed with learning how to become an expert interrogator. My training included a detective course at Ontario Police College that included advanced interrogation rules of evidence. I learned from mentors. I volunteered to write a case law book for my detective office. I studied as much psychology as possible in university. I taught it and wrote about it. But it all started in the uniform patrol branch. Nothing was better than doing it, as a uniform officer, shift-by-shift, call-after-call, traffic stop-after-traffic stop. Formal interrogation happens in a room at a police station but frontline interrogations are the building blocks.

Outside of Hollywood, star interrogators are not born. They're made. They're developed through a long, painful process of high and lows during practice and by putting into practice. Contrary to popular belief, there are no rookie wonders who can step into the role of "star interrogator." During my twenty-year college law-enforcement teaching career, I heard all sorts of delusion from college freshmen/women – *I want to be a detective, I want to be a forensics expert, I want to work undercover… everything except I want to be a uniform patrol officer.* I lost count of how many times I had to burst bubbles and explain real-life to them – *you need to spend a lot of time on the frontline.* Translation: not just any time, quality time. You have to start in the uniform branch, you have to spend many years on frontline patrol where you learn the true fundamentals of investigative strategy, and then you have to compete for advancement with all the other officers who work just as hard as you or even harder.

Most college students didn't want to hear the truth because the truth truly can be painful. The police rookie sensation is the same fictional character as Santa Claus and the Easter Bunny. Developing interrogation expertise is a process that starts the moment your swearing-in ceremony wraps up and the pictures are posted on Facebook, and travels a very slow journey. Every domestic, every disturbance, every death you respond to, every drunk driver, every speeder you stop is another step toward interrogation expertise. Enjoy the ride because you can't press rewind. There's no instant replay on a uniform career.

I spent nine years in uniform and I still miss it. Sacred memories. If you're in uniform, slow down. Don't be in a hurry to get out after a couple of years. Soak it all in. Put aside wild ambitions of instant career gratification and let professional nature take its course. I've taught college students to change their perspective of instant gratification from the all-or-nothing detective badge to the inner reward of the journey by getting better call-by-call. Nothing beats practical real-life experience. Interrogation expertise doesn't just happen.

Nothing just happens. Not overnight or accidentally or randomly. It happens for reason. We make it happen or don't. Fucking things up is part of the learning process. A big part. The key is to investigate every failure. Coaching football taught me the power of studying losing. Studying losing is the key to winning in any profession, by whatever definition you attach to it. My definition of winning is simple – calling out your best. Doing the best job for those who are counting on it. Consistent high-performance. It's the mark of a true professional – full-out, flawless execution, full-time. Anything less and you're disrespecting the profession, disrespecting the citizens and victims who depend on your professionalism, disrespecting your team, and disrespecting yourself. Half-assed, low-performance, bungling amateurism is a disservice to your true boss – the taxpayers.

Point #5:   Confessions don't just happen either.

Being pissed off motivates all crime. Pissed off at self, pissed off at someone else, pissed off at the world, pissed off at being broke, pissed off at things not going one's way. Jealousy, hatred, frustration, bitterness. The same inner conflict that promotes crime, produces a true confession. That's the basic fundamental that governs interrogation psychology – crime and confessions are both attempts to solve an inner conflict. A true confession is the resolution of inner conflict. Crime always fails get the job done, making the inner conflict worse.

Sometimes a suspect will confess instantly. Sometimes it takes time. But no true confession just happens. Every true confession happens *for* a reason and *because of* a reason. The main reason is to end an inner fight caused by Cognitive dissonance[1] and replace it with inner peace. There are two paths to peace – confession or rationalization. Both work. Both do the trick. Both bring peace. But only a true confession brings lasting peace. Rationalization is a band-aid solution that can't stop the bleeding forever. Rationalization can cover up a scratch but it will never fully heal a wound. Confession stops the inner fight before it knocks you out.

Cognitive dissonance is the interrogator's strongest partner. It is an inner conflict caused by acting contrary to personal beliefs. In other words, inconsistency – believing one thing but doing another. Cognitive dissonance is a type of guilt that, left unchecked, turns into a burning inner hell that takes a toll on the soul, torturing the soul in an attempt to kill it off for good. Every human being has a natural desire to be guilt-free. Peace is not just a dream; it's a basic survival need. Spilling your guts saves you from rotting your guts. Cognitive dissonance is unnatural; peace is natural. Cognitive dissonance makes *true* confessions happen naturally. True confession is a homeopathic remedy for a tortured soul, an all-natural cure generated internally. All it takes is pressing the right switch – appeal to the conscience.

---

1   Festinger, Leon. (1957). *A Theory of Cognitive Dissonance*. Stanford, CA: Stanford University Press.

Point #6:   The way to weaken the defence is to score points.

Another challenge of interrogation is overcoming the *presumption of guilt* against the police – that suspicion of wrongdoing that so often hangs over your head when you walk into an interrogation room, do your job right and walk out with a true confession from suspect. It can easily put you on the defensive.

My detective partner and I interrogated a suspect for one break and enter. He confessed to a total of 17 crimes – more break and enters, robberies, and thefts. Then he gave up three of his accomplices for even more crimes. It happened almost in record-breaking time. Short, sweet and to the point. It was the kind of interrogation that contradicted point #3 above – it was too easy. We did nothing special. There was no prolonged questioning. The suspect cleared his conscience almost immediately, without a lot of work. Every detective experiences that kind of no-brainer true confession, the kind where the suspect does all the work and you get credit for it. The kind that reminds you of how simple it can be to get the truth. The kind that makes you believe that it will always be easy, but of course, it won't.

The next night, a uniform officer phoned me at my desk from the uniform briefing room. The officer gave up the patrol sergeant doing the briefing; told me he had announced the results of our interrogation to an entire platoon of uniform officers and implied that we beat the confessions out the suspect. I immediately went to the briefing room, told the patrol sergeant personally that he lied, told the platoon that the patrol sergeant lied, and told the platoon the truth about exactly what had happened. I told the patrol sergeant that if I was victim of any more false allegations, I would sue him.

False allegations are serious business that needs to be corrected instantly. They can't be tolerated because tolerance rewards, empowers, and encourages the liar to do it again. Others will follow. This was a perfect example of the severity of the presumption of guilt – it invades your own team. False allegations are expected by the people you arrest but not from your own team. The cleanest interrogation was tainted by lies that unjustifiably raised doubt about the voluntariness of the confession. That's how easy it is to raise doubt – a few words.

Coaching football taught me several important lessons that relate directly to interrogation and the presumption of guilt:

The defence doesn't just want to stop you, they want you to drop out. They want to break your will so you stop trying. They want to change the way you work so you live in the darkness of fear and doubt. The same applies in law enforcement. The key is focusing on doing your job better than they do.

Never forget that the defence has the easiest job – raising doubt. The police and prosecution have the toughest job – erasing doubt. Don't take it personal, don't make it personal. Raising doubt is simple because it's part of human nature to doubt – to doubt self, to doubt others. Erasing doubt takes evidence. Building a case. A case of hardcore, overwhelming, honest, truthful evidence.

The defence wants to win before the game even starts. The defence wants to score points before the court proceedings begin. They have the presumption of guilt on their side. They want the presumption of your guilt to raise the doubt level about your interrogation/confession before the trial starts. Often, they have help from the media to cast a shadow over your your morals, your ethics and your integrity. The more psychological work they do before court, the less they have to do during court.

Don't fight the defense, score points. Everyone has a role in the criminal justice system. Your job is to score points with evidence. The defence tries to shut you out. Build the strongest case possible by stacking one piece of evidence onto another. Every piece of evidence scores a point. Run up the score. Don't complain about losing when you haven't scored enough points.

Point # 7:   High credibility rating, high return.

Personal credibility is the most forgotten element affecting confession admissibility. Expertise won't save you if no one believes you. Bad reputation, bad return. The biggest investment you can make in your career is scoring a high credibility rating.

Your personal credibility is just as important as any interrogation strategy. A fact that's easy to forget in the swamp of endless case law is that your personal credibility is directly connected to the admissibility or exclusion of a confession. The problem is that high credibility rating doesn't just happen, and it's not permanent, not guaranteed, not proportionate. The presumption of interrogation guilt can make you feel that you're always fighting an uphill battle for credibility, but the truth can stand up to any attack.

High credibility rating is built over time with evidence. You won't get awarded instant high credibility by default. You've got to score a lot of points to get a high credibility score. Then you have to work to sustain it. There's no promise that you will be deemed credible for your entire career because losing points is easier and happens faster than scoring points. Protecting your credibility is investment protection. Guard the points you accumulate because all it takes is one bad play and your score plummets. If your credibility drops, you've got a long road back. This magnifies the severity of the presumption of guilt – your credibility always has an opponent. The bad news is that there's always a fight for your credibility. The good news is that you can go undefeated with the right work.

Lifting and lowering your credibility rating boils down to a war of words, a battle to win the minds of those in charge of passing judgment. Part of the police job description is target practice. You're a target for false allegations, for lies. This is not a "you-against-the-world" speech. Far from it. I've experienced it first-hand, just like you have, in frontline law enforcement. It's just real-life. You're a target for lies because it's part of the fight for the truth.

Point #8:   I call it "interrogation" instead of "interview" for a reason. I replaced "elicit" with "search."

I've been advised to call this series "investigative interviewing" to make it sound politically correct but I can't because the Supreme Court of Canada uses the word "interrogation." For example: The S.C.C. uses the word "interrogation" a total of 130 times in two landmark cases: (i) *R. v. McCrimmon* (2010)[2]; (ii) *R. v. Oickle* (2000).[3] There's nothing wrong with the word interrogation. That's what questioning a suspect for the purpose of getting a true confession is called. Interviews are for witnesses and job candidates. Exploratory interviews are intended to figure out who is a suspect and who isn't. If "interrogation" is a bad label it's because the presumption of guilt is winning the fight.

Some true confessions happen without any interrogation – the suspect confesses instantly, all on his/her own, without any questioning or effort by the police. Most true confessions won't happen that easy. They need to

---

2   http://S.C.C..lexum.org/decisia-S.C.C.-csc/S.C.C.-csc/S.C.C.-csc/en/item/7878/index.do?r=AAAAAQATaW50ZXJyb2dhdGlvbiBncm FudAAAAAAAAE
3   http://S.C.C..lexum.org/decisia-S.C.C.-csc/S.C.C.-csc/S.C.C.-csc/en/item/1801/index.do?r=AAAAAQATaW50ZXJyb2dhdGlvbiBncm FudAAAAAAAAE

be searched for. I used to use the word "elicit" but I've replaced it with "search." Finding citizens who an offender has confessed to needs a "search." "Getting" or "obtaining" a true confession is slang for "searching" – search the conscience for the truth. Confessions are unique evidence because they are composed entirely of words. Like breath samples and blood samples, words are self-incriminating evidence that emerge from the body and like all other evidence, they have to be searched for.

Point #9:   The difference between success and failure is what's given up.

Quadruple meaning: The difference between success and failure by whatever definition you chose depends on:

    i.   how easy you give up;

    ii. what bad habits you give up;

    iii. what the suspect gives up;

    iv. who the suspect gives up.

It's easy to give up when something seems too tough to do. It's easy to do a job wrong instead of doing it right. It's easy to lie about the truth and lie to protect others, especially if you've been conditioned to do this in the past.

This is not a book about how to get a confession at any cost. It's a book about giving up – what to give up and what not to give up. It's about how to get the truth to make sure you've got the right guy, to make sure you never get the wrong guy, and to make sure that the victims and the public get in return what they've given up – tax dollars, trust, and hope.

Point #10:   The reason I wrote this book was to make a difference.

"... the exact scope of the Confessions Rule has been the subject of debate over the past century..."

                              – Supreme Court of Canada[4]

"The law concerning the voluntariness of statements, made by accused persons, to a person in authority, has not always been a model of clarity."

                              – Justice M. Dambrot, Ontario Superior Court of Justice[5]

Let those two statements sink in. Take a moment and re-read them. They are understatements about how complex and confusing interrogation laws are in Canada. Confession and interrogation laws have been "debated" for over 100 years. They have not been a "model of clarity." It's not an exaggeration to call it chaos. But it's easy for lawyers, judges, and the media to criticize the police who have to make split-second decisions to apply this mess of laws on the frontlines. It's truly hard to believe, but the police are the only ones in the entire criminal justice system who have to unclutter the clutter with rapid-fire decisions. Everyone else does after-the-fact analysis. The police are the only ones who face the test head- on. Everyone else marks the test with the 20/20 vision of hindsight.

---

4   R. v. Hebert (1990) 57 C.C.C. (3d) 1 (S.C.C.).
5   R. v. Dalzell (2003) CanLII 49355 (ON S.C.).

The system is set up for police failure. Here's what I mean - the academic playing field is extremely tilted. Academic imbalance. Judges, defence lawyers, and prosecutors all have law degrees. Most police officers don't. Policing education doesn't compare with that of the rest of the CJS. Interrogation education and training is nowhere near what it needs to be to balance the playing field. I can make a strong argument that interrogation expertise needs an undergraduate psychology degree and a graduate degree in law. And more higher learning in communication, leadership, and interpersonal relationship skills.

I used to complain that interrogation laws work against the police. *The bad guy gets all the breaks. The bad guy has all the advantages.* Not true. I was narrow-minded. I didn't see the truth until I pursued my education. Complaining about interrogation laws was the equivalent of complaining that my football team should be allowed to jump offside, interfere or hold, just to make it easier to win. The bottom-line is that developing investigative and interrogation expertise takes unwavering commitment to continuing education. It takes a passion for life-long learning.

I've changed careers from police officer to college law-enforcement professor to business owner and football coach but I never stopped being a citizen, father, grandfather, and taxpayer. Like many Canadians, my family has been affected by life-threatening crime. My motivation for writing this book is to help balance the academic playing field and to help with the public safety fight. My motivation is to help officers juggle their careers and personal lives with life-long learning because there's no greater social challenge than public safety. If we can't protect our citizens, we have a big problem because no other social institution will work well.

Based on personal experience, I know how difficult it is to research interrogation laws, how difficult it is to learn and understand them, and how difficult it is to get it right in the interrogation room and then in court. This book is my attempt to help make it less difficult. My writing style is simple – I don't preach, I teach… myself. I talk to myself. I use the word "you" throughout the book for two reasons: (i) it's worked in my other textbooks to make them less academically boring; (ii) "you" also means, "me." Not one word in this book is directed at you per se. I write to myself and share it with the intention of trying to make difference in a world that sorely needs it.

Peace.

Gino Arcaro

Part I: The Basics

Chapter 1
Triple Play

There are three case law rulings that set the focus for interrogation and confessions. These are three case law statements that build the base for interrogation ideology and strategy right off the bat. They prove *value, right, purpose* – the evidentiary value of a confession, the right to interrogate, and the purpose of an interrogation. This triple play of case law defends and justifies interrogation ethics while providing the starting point of interrogation strategy.

Value: *"Confessions are among the most useful types of evidence. Where freely and voluntarily given, an admission of guilt provides a reliable tool in the elucidation of crime, thereby furthering the judicial search for the truth and serving the societal interest in repressing crime through the conviction of the guilty."*

– Supreme Court of Canada[6]

This statement is strong enough to prioritize investigative objectives by making the search for a true confession made to *anyone* as the central focus of any investigation. Not the only priority, the top priority. True confessions made to *anyone* should be at the top of the investigative objective list because no evidence is stronger. There are several types of strong evidence but a true confession has a special place in a league of its own. It's the reason why, *"Did s/he confess?"* is at the top of the list of questions asked when an arrest is made in a major crime. A true confession is generally viewed as the definitive proof of guilt. A true confession is not the end of an investigation but it ends any doubt about whether the right or wrong person was arrested and charged.

A confession **to the police** can be the most valuable evidence in any case because it can remove all doubt about guilt in the minds of judges and jurors if it passes three tests:

    i.   voluntary/reliability

    ii. Charter credibility, and

    iii. testimony credibility.

A confession **to a citizen** has even higher value because it has to pass only the credibility test. These tests are the equivalent of forensic tests for physical evidence.

Since true confessions are the most valuable evidence, it stands to reason that interrogation is the number one investigative skill since it should result in a true confession. Interrogation expertise should be at the top of the training goals for any officer who wants to become a detective or wants to make a career as a patrol officer.

Of all the investigative skills, none are more important and more challenging to learn and develop than interrogation. Training and practical experience. Education and action. The secret to developing interrogation expertise is *R.E.P.S. – Repeatedly Experience Practical Skills.*

---

6   R. v. Smith (1989) 50 C.C.C. (3d) 308 (S.C.C.) at 324.

Right to interrogate: *"A police officer is entitled to question any person whether reasonable grounds or mere suspicion exists, to determine whether an offence has been committed or who committed it."*

– Ontario Court of Appeal[7]

This statement answers simple, basic questions:

1. Do the police need reasonable grounds to formally or informally interrogate a person? No.

2. Can the police interrogate on mere suspicion? Yes.

3. Does this rule apply to the frontline as well as the formal interrogation room? Yes.

4. Can you force a person to answer your questions? No.

The right to ask questions is simple and basic although we're all governed by the laws of human decency and professionalism. You don't have to make apologies for asking interrogation questions, formally or informally when talking to a suspect or accused person or trying to make a list of suspects or confirming/deleting them from the suspect list. Accordingly, it's not illegal, immoral, or unethical to ask, for example, "Did you rob that store? " or, "Why did you break into that place?" You don't need reasonable grounds to ask a question. If the person doesn't want to answer, they have the right to remain silent. Of course, there's a strategic time and place to ask direct formal and informal interrogation questions but my point is that this case law rule is a basic fundamental to remember when you doubt yourself about whether you have the right to ask questions. The time and place to ask direct questions does need strategic purpose but never forget you have the right to ask questions without reasonable grounds, especially if you're on the frontline responding to a life-and-death emergency. The right to ask questions is a legal and ethical strategy to develop proper suspicion or confirm/eliminate it. But always remember that you can't force an answer. Unlike a demand for a breath sample, there's no demand for "answers" in Canadian law.

Purpose: *"Hopefully, admissions of guilt in such a context may contribute to the person's rehabilitation and reintegration into society as a responsible individual."*

– Supreme Court of Canada[8]

This is a powerful message – the purpose of a confession is the redeeming quality of the confession, a benefit for both the offender and the public. Print this and carry it with you. Show it to suspects during interrogations. It's not an inducement to teach a suspect what the law states about the redeeming quality of a confession and it will do the job of appealing to the suspect's conscience. Emphasize the two key words - *rehabilitation and reintegration.*

According to this statement, you should be applauded every time a suspect gives you a true confession. The criminal justice system and society in general should commend you for starting the rehabilitation and reintegration process. When the media, lawyers, or anyone else questions your motives for interrogation, recite this statement made by the Supreme Court of Canada verbatim. Memorize it. Cite the case – *R. v. Smith* (1989) 2 SCR 368. Handout printed copies of the quote. Be sincere. Don't be a smart ass. Mean it straight from the heart. The purpose of interrogation, according the S.C.C., is to help rehabilitate and reintegrate the offender. If you don't try to interrogate a suspect, you're actually neglectful. If the offender doesn't confess, you've failed to help the offender and society. The rehabilitation and reintegration process is stalled without a confession. You can go one step further – confession is spiritual reconciliation. It heals the soul. Repairing the soul is the biggest part of the rehabilitation process.

---

7   R .v. Moran (1987) 36 C.C.C. (3d) 225 (ONT.CA).
8   R. v. Smith (1989) 50 C.C.C. (3d) 308 (S.C.C.) at 324.

This S.C.C. statement of purpose implies the following:

1. Questioning a suspect is an *expectation*. It is part of the police function. It's their job. They are expected to question potential suspects and determine the truth for the purpose of starting the rehabilitation and reintegration process.

2. A true, voluntary confession is a *change agent* and vital for social improvement.

3. True, voluntary confessions are a *crime prevention* strategy. They are *proactive public safety strategy*. A rehabilitated offender won't become a recidivist. Preventing crime is the primary aim of law enforcement. A confession is a fast, cost-effective method that enables offenders to become productive members of society.

4. The *absence* of a confession means multiple benefits are lost. Not trying to get a confession or failing to get one costs the offender and the public in potential recidivism.

Here's the first lesson in interrogation strategy – state the purpose. Inform the suspect why you're questioning him or her. Teach the suspect the redeeming benefits of confessing. Include the source – the Supreme Court of Canada. It's not an illegal inducement to tell the truth by teaching law and stating a fact. There's no illegal promise or threat by telling a suspect that the top court in the country stated that a confession can rehabilitate and reintegrate. And it accomplishes the goal of all interrogation strategy – appeal to the conscience and trigger the inner compulsion to confess.

When should you tell the suspect? At what point of the interrogation should you invoke this statement? The answer is found in the "strategize and improvise" decision-making model. Build a general plan before you start the interrogation and adapt to the unexpected and ever-changing circumstances of any conversation, including interrogation. Don't wing it but don't script it. Analyze your case. What are the strengths and weakness of your evidence? What factors will appeal directly to this specific suspect?

Here are your options – open with the Court's statement or choose to delay it. The first option is to use it as the first play, the primary strategy that opens the interrogation. Tell the suspect right off the bat exactly what the S.C.C. said. This can set the tone by building the right focus – away from external consequences. The right focus is for the suspect to solve his/her most immediate problem – guilt. Cognitive dissonance – the growing pressure of inner conflict that, left unchecked, will explode into an inner hell. That focus is what triggers the *self-generated confession*, the type of confession that the S.C.C. has ruled passes the voluntary/ reliability test for confession admissibility.

The second option is use the rehabilitation/reintegration strategy as backup – inform the suspect of it after other strategies have built the interrogation base. Your choice is part of the decision-making process that characterizes every interrogation. All dialogue, including interrogation, is a series of decisions made about what to ask, what to answer, and what to comment on. Every word spoken and all silence during an interrogation is a product of a decision, consciously or subconsciously made. Nothing just happens during an interrogation. Nothing is said randomly. Every word spoken and all silence is decided through habit, the hardwiring of thought and speech created through repeated practice until it becomes second-nature communication – speech fingerprint. Listen to yourself closely. Pay attention to how you converse casually and how you question anybody, professionally or privately. You'll find predictable patterns – speech DNA that positively identifies you. Or negatively identifies you. It all depends on what type of impact you make on your audience – positive or negative.

You can do the same with your audience. Listen to those involved in your conversation. Paying attention will identify habitual speech patterns that reveal the person's inner workings – mind, heart, soul. What we say shows what we think. How we say it shows how we think.

The decision to use any interrogation strategy depends on the conclusions drawn from pre-interrogation analytics – what strategy will appeal the fastest and the strongest to the offender's conscience? What will make the biggest impact on the offender's compulsion to confess, triggering the inner urge to reconcile cognitive dissonance by telling the truth? The "strategize & improvise" approach will build a general plan and develop the ability to adapt while the interrogation is in progress. Scripted interrogations are inflexible and can't predict the outcome of every question/comment. Winging it won't work out because unstructured dialogue misses the target due to randomness – no aim, no direction.

Delivering the rehabilitation/reintegration case law statement will generate an outcome. It may generate a verbal response or silence but it will strike a chord if you get the message across. *Striking the chord* is the goal of every interrogation strategy. Appealing to the conscience and triggering the inner compulsion to confess using the all-natural approach – setting in motion the inner sense of right and wrong. Every true confession happens after the chord is struck. No exception. Instant confessions and delayed confessions all happen after the chord is struck. Every investigator has hardcore evidence of how many people an offender has told about wrongdoing without any interrogation prompting whatsoever. The volume of confessions made to citizens (persons not-in-authority) is overwhelming proof that the inner urge to confess is a force of nature that works without any police questioning. Conversely, offenders don't confess when the chord is not struck, when the conscience is not relied on to work out the problem.

How many times you use the same play depends on rapid-fie analysis of the outcome. The number of times you say the same thing depends on whether it is working or not. Confessions are solution to two problems – misconduct and guilt, the chain reaction between wrongdoing and paying the price internally. You'll never go wrong by repeating what the S.C.C. has taught us about the connection between confession and rehabilitation/ reintegration.

How many different ways can you effectively, legally, and morally say the same thing? Plenty. Be creative, speak from the heart, and combine other important strategies, especially emphasise the connection between choice/free will and truth/honesty, for example:

- Telling the truth is life-changing. It's your choice.

- Telling the truth is the first step to rehabilitation, to becoming a productive member of society. You control that choice.

- Telling the truth is the moral way to heal what needs to be healed. You control the decision.

- Nothing changes inside us until we tell the truth. It's completely up to you.

- The first step in changing ourselves is telling the truth. No one can force you to tell the truth. No one can force you to change.

- Nothing changes inside ourselves as long as we keep bullshitting ourselves. Note: street-talk has a purpose. Street-talk is the official language in many places. I've never read a case law decision that directly bans profanity. But, case law is clear about the context – the big picture. How words like 'bullshit' are perceived depends on the context, specifically how it affected the suspect's free will.

There's a line that you can't cross. Street-talk benefits include speaking at the level of the suspect's sophistication. Contrary to popular myth, interrogation rooms don't pit saints versus sinners. Social values have changed. Words like 'bullshit' are not considered gratuitous obscenity in every social world. How can we condemn street-talk when it has become the official language in some social circles? Street-talk does have a purpose as long as you don't cross the line.

- The first step in rehabilitation is healing the soul. It starts with honesty. Telling the truth is healing. We all have free will. Life is about choices. What we become or don't become is our choice. Its starts with honesty. We can lie to ourselves but don't expect positive change. Self-deception is a trap, a viscous cycle that keeps us the same without moving forward. Telling the truth is powerful. It rehabilitates and helps you get on with your life by reintegrating in society so you can make a positive impact on the world.

None of this is preaching. Coaching football taught me the power of motivational speaking. There's a direct connection between inspirational communication and interrogation. Telling the truth instead of lying requires change. The best way to change people is to give them hope. The best way to convince someone to tell the truth is to teach them about hope and show them a sign of hope as an act of good faith. Hopelessness promotes more of the same. Every time someone has told you the truth, you've lifted their soul. Every time you've told the truth to someone else, they lifted your soul. Believe it. Review your past interrogations. Whether you're a uniform officer or detective, analyze your past and you'll find common ground – soul-lifting.

Healing the soul makes a powerful impact on any guilty offender. Anyone who is carrying the burden of a crime needs to relieve the inner hell of guilt. In the same case as the reintegration comment, *R. v. Smith* (1989), the S.C.C. added the following statement:

*"There is nothing inherently wrong with the taking of a statement from a person who feels the **need** to <u>relieve guilt pressures</u> and who therefore waives his right to counsel."*

The S.C.C. made it clear – "relieving guilt pressure" is real. It's an inner motivation for offenders to confess. It's not a "want," it is a "need." But needs are not created equal. There are ordinary needs and there are ones that you can't live without – basic survival needs. When guilt turns up the pressure, relieving it becomes a basic survival need – much more than an ordinary need. The reason is that guilt is painful. Pain is distracting. It gets in the way of peace, breaking focus on what we want to do with our lives. Getting rid of guilt is a top priority because it blocks the peace and happiness that we make a life out of striving for. And most importantly, "there is nothing inherently wrong" with the strategy of emphasizing that "need" by taking a confession from the suspect. Relieving guilt pressure is part of the soul-healing process. It's part of the interrogation **intangibles** – what works behind-the-scenes can't always be seen. The intangibles are what makes interrogation challenging and controversial. What can't be seen becomes a mystery. Mysteries are filled with uncertainties. Uncertainties promote one of the worst types of fear – fear of the unknown. Fear it, criticize it. The controversy surrounding interrogation stems from fear of the intangibles that remain unknown to the uninformed.

The Triple Play case law is the starting point of the ethical interrogation mindset. High-performance of any skill starts at the top with the right mindset. In this case, the right mindset is to adopt the case law thinking – think exactly like Canadian courts think. Speak the message of Canadian courts by translating it into ordinary language during every interrogation. It's the simple common-sense approach – follow the leader. It's the defence mechanism that silences the critics. Crisis management through case law management.

The Triple Play shows that true confessions are a solution to two problems – misconduct and guilt: the chain reaction between wrongdoing and paying the price internally. You'll never go wrong by maintaining that perspective – an interrogation is meant to be a problem-solver not a means to condemn. Interrogation is a solution to the problem of misconduct and guilt, not a punishment. Telling the truth is a natural pain-reliever, not a pain-inducer. Critics won't call interrogation "psychological manipulation" when you speak the case law language of Canadian courts. They'll call it "necessary."

Chapter 2
Rules of Evidence: Adult Confession Admissibility – The Truth Test

How do you know you've scored a goal if the contest rules are buried in the referee's decision which is written and stored at the league office instead of in an easily accessible all-encompassing hard-copy rulebook? How do you do your job if you don't know where the white lines are? If you have to guess where the sidelines are, how do you stay in bounds?

In a perfect world, there would be one statute that would include and explain everything you need to know about how to get a true confession from an adult suspect and how to prove what needs to be proved to ensure its admissibility. There isn't a perfect world or such a statute in Canada. The Rules of Evidence that govern adult confession admissibility are spread out in various sources of Canadian law, creating a nightmare research project to investigate them.

The following diagram is a snapshot of the basic rules related to adult confession admissibility. The X shows two paths that cross to form the "Truth Test" – how to test a confession for a positive match with the truth. Words are a unique type of evidence. They emerge from a human body the same as other substance such as blood samples and breath samples but unlike these bodily substances, there is no scientific test to match words to the truth. The Truth Test is the equivalent of forensic testing for physical evidence. It analyzes the words that make up a confession. A confession has to be tested for the truth and a positive match made for it to be of any evidentiary value.

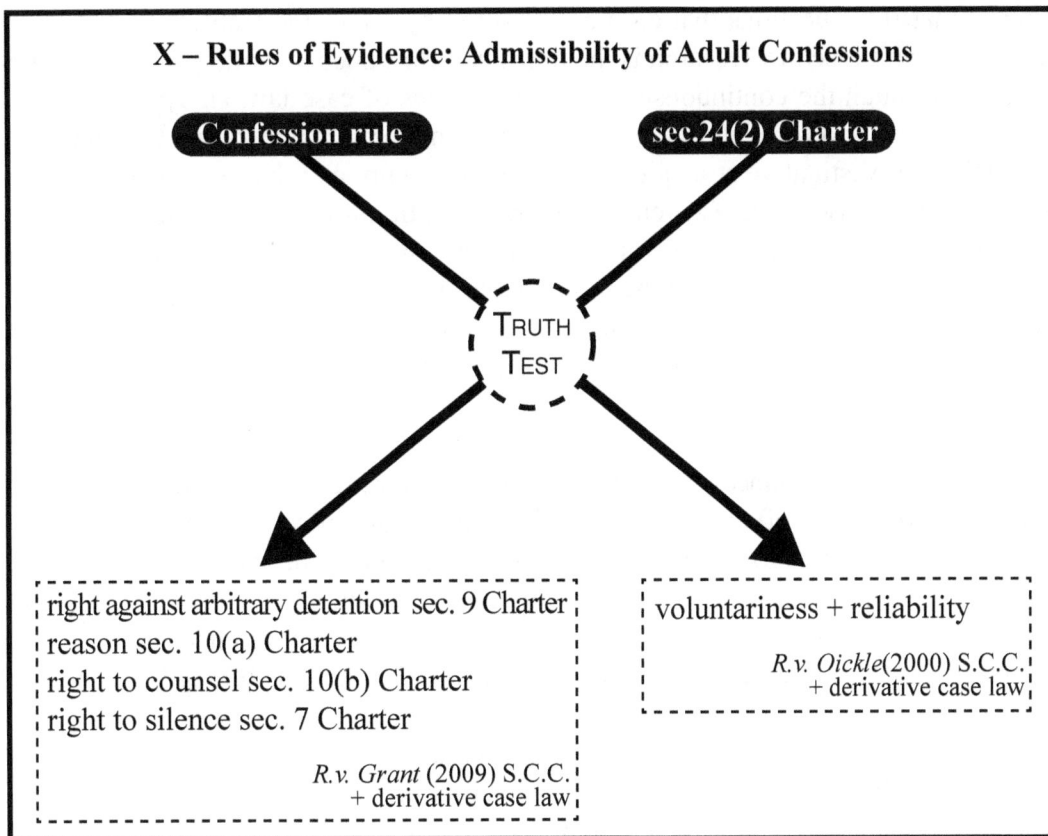

X – Rules of Evidence: Admissibility of Adult Confessions

Confession rule   **sec.24(2) Charter**

TRUTH TEST

right against arbitrary detention sec. 9 Charter
reason sec. 10(a) Charter
right to counsel sec. 10(b) Charter
right to silence sec. 7 Charter

R.v. Grant (2009) S.C.C.
+ derivative case law

voluntariness + reliability

R.v. Oickle(2000) S.C.C.
+ derivative case law

∞

The X shows the connection between the two pathways of laws that govern adult confession admissibility:

i.   the "Confessions Rule" found in common law and case law, and

ii. sec. 24(2) Charter.

Neither law explains concrete guidelines about how to get a true confession. They do explain the required outcome but not the process. The Confessions Rule creates the onus for the police/prosecution to prove voluntary/reliability, while sec. 24(2) Charter creates the obligation for the police to prevent Charter violations designed to protect the rights guaranteed to suspects/accused persons. The combined effect of both laws explains when confessions are thrown out and when they're safe. Confessions are thrown out when the words were involuntary/unreliable or when the words were said to the police after a Charter violation was committed (and the admission would jeopardize the reputation of the criminal justice system). In other words, confessions are thrown out when words are forced out of a person or when a penalty preceded them. A confession is safe when it's free and clean – illegal inducement-free and Charter violation-free. A free confession is a clean confession. A clean confession is the truth.

The problem is that both rules are abstract concepts open to wide-ranging interpretations. Neither have concrete definitions or concrete guidelines. Both explain the goal but not the process. Here's an analogy. Imagine a sports rulebook that simply instructed "every touchdown has to be clean" or, "only penalty-free goals are allowed" without any clear instruction about to accomplish them cleanly or penalty-free.

Case law research is the solution to the problem of vagueness. Case law provides concrete definitions, and answers specific "What if?" questions that are not answered by either the Confessions Rule or sec. 24 (2) Charter. The difficulty with case law research is the time and effort needed while you're in the field doing the job. You have to sift through the continuously growing volumes of case law, analyze complex legal jargon that characterizes case law, and translate each decision into simple language to find the practical lessons, the ready-to-use in real-life investigative strategies. The current system, as it has always been, is unreasonable. It lacks logic and sense because it's a research nightmare and a training nightmare for law enforcement. The police have to know the same extent of interrogation laws as lawyers and judges but have nowhere near the same time to learn and develop expertise in them. It's ludicrous to believe that the police don't have to have the same knowledge as lawyers and judges. Back to the sports analogy: the referees and the other team know the rules and can score "clean" while you don't know how to accomplish this (and, well, that's the way it's always been, so deal with it).

The current system creates an unbalanced playing field. The how-to rules are not easily accessible. Interrogation rules can't be taught and learned efficiently because the realities of police work prevent police departments from sending officers to extended, long-term courses for higher education. Then there's the issue of practice. Like with any skill, interrogation needs practice and simulated training but it's almost impossible to plan and simulated interrogation. A make-believe offender is not the same as a real offender no matter how good the acting is. You can try hard to replicate the real thing but you won't. There's nothing like the real thing.

Often, interrogation skill development depends on OTJ training – on-the-job training. OTJ training has some benefits but the mistakes inherent to OTJ training have disproportionate consequences in the real-life world of the criminal justice system. There's a steep price to pay for interrogation mistakes. Unlike with traffic violators, where discretion is allowed, there are no breaks given to police officers for interrogation screw-ups; the confession gets thrown out.

Reform is needed. Change isn't an option, it's a necessity. Here's another football analogy – imagine expecting coaches and athletes to research endless referee calls trying to figure out exactly how to legally block, tackle, pass, catch, or, know what the field dimensions are, where the goal line is, where the end zone is, and, what specifically constitutes a touchdown. How can you do your job right if the size of the field changes *after* the game is done or when the rules change *during* the instant replay? In hockey, how can you score a goal if you're not sure where the net is, how big the net is, and if you're shooting the puck correctly? How can you score a goal if no one can agree on what exactly a goal is?

The following two statements are worth repeating from Chapter Zero :

"... the exact scope of the Confessions Rule has been the subject of debate over the past century..."

– Supreme Court of Canada[9]

"The law concerning the voluntariness of statements, made by accused persons, to person in authority, has not always been a model of clarity."

– Justice M. Dambrot, Ontario Superior Court of Justice[10]

Reform is needed to make confession/interrogation laws a "model of clarity." We can't wait for another 100 years of debate. We can't afford another century of pendulum swings. In my opinion, you can't keep stitching together interrogation/confession laws for 100 years hoping that the final product somehow will look like a fine quilt. Concrete laws and guidelines are needed. Otherwise, the same debate will continue for centuries.

∞

When rules cross paths

The two admissibility paths cross on the X for a dual purpose – rules for admissibility and rules for exclusion. The offense and defense playbooks come from the same rulebook. The X represents the playing field but the crossroad in the middle of the X is the most important place on the X. The two paths have to meet for confession admissibility. When the Confessions Rule and the Charter cross paths, the truth works out. The farther apart they are, the truth won't happen or the truth will never be heard because it will be silenced through exclusion.

The interplay of voluntariness and Charter right is a security plan that protects both the suspect and the police. Both the suspect and police need protection from wrongful accusation. It's not a one-way street. The truth is a two-way street. When the two-way streets meet at the crossroads of the X, everyone is protected. The farther apart they are, security fails – there's no protection.

There are two ways to look at this chart – limits or leeway. The conventional way of looking at the X connection is with the phrase *limits of interrogations*. Law literature often refers to the limits of interrogation as a form of brainwashing to divert and hide the leeway afforded to the police. Using the word, "limits" is an attempt to condition your mind to focus on restrictions that make limitations seem more constrictive than they really are. What you focus on grows. Focus on the limits and the limits grow. Limits are all you'll see. Open your mind to limits and you will see leeway – legal, ethical leeway that lets you do your job. On the flip side, it's easy to focus so much on leeway that you forget the limits. Tunnel vision on the leeway of case law runs the risk of ignoring the limits altogether. The key is to strike the balance – see both. Respect the limits but don't let limits shackle you. Respect leeway but don't exploit it, don't take advantage by believing you're entitled to break interrogation laws because it's too hard to get a confession.

---

9   R. v. Hebert (1990) 57 C.C.C. (3d) 1 (S.C.C.).
10   R. v. Dalzell (2003) CanLII 49355 (ON S.C.).

In reality, there's a balance between limits of interrogation and leeway of interrogation. There's a danger in both underestimating and overestimating both the limits and the leeway. The limits don't prohibit the police from doing their job. Overestimating the limits obstructs the highest performance you're capable of. And you'll fall in the same trap that I did, by complaining that the laws are all against the police and in favour of the offender. The police have more than enough leeway to work with. Misinterpreting the limits will prevent you from using the full extent of leeway that the law gives to the police. Conversely, confusing limits with leeway exposes you to consequences ranging from exclusion of evidence to civil and criminal liability. The secret is *continuing education.* Commit yourself to "case law higher education." Never stop learning. Make a conscious decision to become a case law expert. Knowledge is more than power. It's a basic survival need. Without knowledge, you don't stand a chance in your profession or any profession. Without knowledge, you're making it easier for the competition to win. Yes, the defence is the competition. The words "competition" and "winning" are not politically incorrect or dangerous or immoral or unethical. "Winning" is a catch-all phrase that represents doing your job better than your competition. It means bringing out your very best consistently, without excuses. That's why they always have and always will call it "winning the case." Without high-level knowledge, you're making the competition's job easy. And not knowing enough is a disservice to crime victims, it disrespects the public, the criminal justice system, and the profession of law enforcement. It's impossible to discern leeway from limits without becoming a case law expert. Stretch goal: Learn more about case law than anyone else.

Chapter 3
Language

Interrogation laws have a language. There are a number of words and definitions that emerge from, and are relevant to the Rules of Evidence that govern confession admissibility. The following is a glossary of 35 basic definitions – the fundamentals of Rules of Evidence language:

Glossary

1. Suspect[11]: A person linked to a criminal offence by concrete evidence that forms a belief below reasonable grounds but more than speculation. The level of belief is the same that justifies investigative detention, formerly called "articulable cause" and re-named "reasonable suspicion."[12]

2. Accused person[13]: Two definitions. The first is found in sec. 493 Criminal Code. The second emerges from case law:

    i.   Sec. 493 C.C.: A person arrested for a criminal offence or a person to whom a peace officer has issued an appearance notice under sec. 496 C.C.

    ii. A person formally charged by being named in a sworn Information.

An accused person is connected by a reasonable grounds belief to a criminal offence. If reasonable grounds exists that a person has committed a criminal offence, the person qualifies as an "accused person" whether an Information has been laid or has not yet been laid.

3. Person in Authority[14] (PIA): A person in authority is defined as either:

    i.   Any person engaged in the arrest, detention, interrogation or prosecution of the accused person, or;

    ii. any person whom the accused person/suspect reasonably believes is acting on behalf of the state and could influence or control the proceedings against him or her favourably or negatively.

The list includes, but is not limited to police officers, prosecutors, and correctional workers.

4. Person *not* in Authority[15] (PNIA): A person not in authority is defined as either:

    i.   Any person *not* engaged in the arrest, detention, interrogation or prosecution of the accused person, or;

    ii. any person whom the accused person/suspect reasonably believes is *not* acting on behalf of the state and *cannot* influence or control the proceedings against him or her favourably or negatively.

The list includes, but is not limited to, *citizens* (non-peace officers). A citizen may become a PIA depending on the situation and what the suspect believes.

---

11   R. v. Dalzell (2003) CanLII 49355 (ON S.C.).
12   R. v. Mann[2004] S.C.C., 3 S.C.R. 59.
13   Ibid.
14   R. v. Hodgson (1998) S.C.C., 127 C.C.C. (3d) 449; R. v. A.B.(1986) Ont. C.A., 26 C.C.C. (3d) 17.
15   Ibid.

5. Statement: Any type of communication made by a suspect or accused person, out of court, to any person.

   - "Any type of communication" means written, verbal, or non-verbal.

   - "Non-verbal" means conduct (acts or gestures) including, but not limited to, nodding or shaking the head and shrugging the shoulders.

   - "Out of court" means *before* the trial. Statements *during* the trial constitute "testimony," a different concept.

   - "Statement" means pre-trial communication by a suspect or an accused that occurs *during* the *investigation*.

   - "Any person" means PIA and/or PNIA.

6. Inculpatory statement: Incriminating statement.

7. Exculpatory statement: Denial or alibi.

8. Admission: An inculpatory statement that proves at least one fact-in-issue but not all the facts-in-issue. A partial confession, e.g., a statement that proves intent but not actus reus, or, any one fact-in-issue of an offence but not all facts-in-issue.

9. Confession: An inculpatory statement that proves all the facts-in-issue. An inculpatory statement that constitutes a prima facie case, e.g., "I did it," (as a response to questioning).

10. Voir Dire: An admissibility hearing. Conducted during the trial to determining whether evidence, i.e., a confession, will be admissible or excluded. Traditionally called a "trial within a trial," it really means a "*hearing* within a trial."

11. Interview: Questioning a witness, a non-suspect, or a potential suspect to explore the truth.

12. Interrogation: Questioning a suspect or accused person with a goal of eliciting a true confession or inculpatory statement.

13. Inducement: The cause or reason for a confession; the influence, incentive, persuasion, or catalyst that produces a confession.

14. *Improper* inducement: A quid pro quo offer, made by a person in authority, of a *threat* or *promise* (in exchange for a confession) that is strong enough to compel an involuntary confession; an illegal inducement.

15. *Proper* inducement: Any inducement by any person that does not constitute a quid pro quo offer or threat or promise, or, a quid pro quo offer *not strong* enough to compel an involuntary confession; a legal inducement that produces a voluntary confession, including a moral inducement – an appeal to the conscience. Includes self-generated pressure caused by guilt to relieve guilt.

16. *Contextual inducement:* An inducement requiring a trial judge's evaluation, within the context of an entire interrogation, to classify the inducement as improper or proper. A contextual inducement may be legal or illegal, depending on how it fits within the entire context of the interrogation.

17. Benefit: A reward. The gaining of an advantage or avoidance of a disadvantage or consequence.

18. Proceedings: A legal process that starts with the laying of an Information and ends with the end of prosecution (end of trial or withdrawal of information).

19. Voluntary: Free from *improper* inducement.

20. Oppression: Inhumane conditions that would motivate a person to falsely confess, purely out of a desire to escape those conditions.

21. Operating mind: A mental capacity permitting a person to voluntarily confess, and that is free from conditions that may cause an involuntary statement. Functional free will.

22. Quid pro Quo: Something for something.[16] A thing given in exchange for something. A quid pro quo offer refers to an offer to give a benefit in return for a confession.[17]

23. False confession: A fabricated confession. A confession made by an innocent person (one who did not commit the offence).

24. True confession: An honest confession. A confession made by a person who actually committed the offence.

25. Reliability: The credibility of a confession relating to truthfulness.

26. Reliable confession: A confession proved to be true, not false.

27. Caution[18]: A non-statutory verbal warning to a suspect or accused that:

    i.   he/she has the right to remain silent, and;

    ii. any statement made by him/her may be admissible in court.

28. Formal caution: A <u>recommended</u> caution that reads: *"Do you wish to say anything in answer to the charge? You are not obliged to say anything unless you wish to do so but whatever you say may be given in evidence."*

29. Right to counsel:

    i.   A statutory-mandated verbal instruction informing a person that he/she has the right to consult with a lawyer.

    ii. A section 10(b) Charter right guaranteed to arrested or detained persons.

The accused may choose to invoke it or waive it.

---

16   Oxford Dictionary.
17   R. v. Oickle (2000), File No. 26535 (S.C.C.).
18   R. v. Dalzell (2003) CanLII 49355 (ON S.C.).

30. Right to silence: A section 7 Charter right that gives suspects or accused persons being questioned by police, the *choice* to answer or not. The accused may choose to invoke or waive the Right.

31. Section 24(2) Charter: The provision that creates the *general* rule of admissibility/exclusion of evidence. One of two rules that govern the admissibility of a confession. Evidence obtained *after* the commission of a Charter violation may either be admissible or excluded. The determining factor is the effect the admissibility or exclusion will have on the reputation of the Criminal Justice System (CJS).

32. Traditional Confessions Rule (a.k.a. Ibrahim Rule): Any statement made by an offender to a PIA before, during, or after an offence is admissible *if* the prosecutor proves the statement was *voluntarily* made.[19] This traditional confession rule, also known as the *Ibrahim Rule,* has been partially transformed to include a *broader* meaning of the "Concept of Voluntary."

33. Contemporary Confessions Rule: A statement made by an offender to a PIA before, during, or after a crime, is admissible if the prosecutor proves that the statement was *voluntary* and *reliable*, within the *context* of the circumstances, considering four factors: (i) threats or promises; (ii) oppression; (iii) operating mind; (iv)trickery.[20] This description represents the modified version of the Confessions Rule with a broader meaning that expands the concept of voluntariness.

34. Confessions Rule: One of the two rules that govern admissibility of a confession. This term represents the most up-to-date version of the rule and is the same as the *Contemporary* Confessions Rule.[21]

35. Police Persuasion: Case law authority that allows the police to interrogate a suspect *after* the Right to Silence has been invoked, for the purpose/intention of breaking the suspect's silence.

---

19   R. v. Oickle (2000), File No. 26535 (S.C.C.).
20   Ibid.
21   R. v. Oickle (2000), File No. 26535 (S.C.C.).

Chapter 4
Basic Confession Rules of Evidence 101

No two people will conduct an interrogation the exact same way. Everyone has to use the same rules of evidence and use the same playbook of interrogation strategies that emerge from them but the efficiency of those strategies will depend on execution – how the strategies are communicated.

The essence of interrogation is communication. Every human has a personalized style of communication, similar to communication DNA or communication fingerprint. Communication style is learned over a lifetime, including how a person learns and is trained in confession rules of evidence. Our personalized communication style is a manifestation of cognitive hardwiring – habits forms by reps. Repetition is the secret behind all performance – high or low, good or bad, expert or half-assed mediocre. The starting point is the basics, how the fundamentals are processed and internalized. Developing effective, legal, ethical interrogation strategy works hand-in-hand with studying Confession Rules of Evidence and the derivative case law that emerges from it. Start developing an interrogation communication style that's compatible with the Confession Rules of Evidence. It's a step-by-step process that begins with the basics: Confession Rules of Evidence 101.

The Confessions Rule and sec. 24(2) Charter are the two basic rules of evidence that work together to form a complex network of advanced rules of evidence that decide whether a confession is admitted at a trial or excluded. The Confessions Rule is specific to confessions while sec 24(2) Charter is a general rule that applies to all types of evidence. A confession to the police <u>will</u> be thrown out if it is involuntary/unreliable and <u>may</u> be thrown out if it follows a Charter violation. The Confessions Rule is absolute, leading to mandatory exclusion – violating the rule *will* exclude a confession to the police. Section 24(2) Charter is not absolute. It is a discretionary exclusion rule. How the courts use discretion will be explained in subsequent chapters as they relate to *R. v. Grant* (2009) S.C.C.,[22] the most recent landmark case law decision that re-defined the sec. 24(2) Charter decision-making model.

The following are the basic two rules of adult confession evidence. An additional rule that governs young offender interrogations and confessions is added – sec 146 *Youth Criminal Justice* (YCJA). It combines elements of the Confessions Rule and sec. 24(2) Charter.

Confessions Rule

> A statement made by an offender to a person in authority before, during, or after a crime is admissible if the prosecutor proves that the statement was *voluntary* and *reliable*, within the *context* of the circumstances, considering four factors: threats or promises, oppression, operating mind, and tricking.[23]
>
> – *R.v.Oickle* (2000) S.C.C.

---

22   R. v. Grant (2009) S.C.C. 32; 2 SCR 353.
23   R. v. Oickle (2000), File No. 26535 (S.C.C.).

24.(2) Where, in proceedings under subsection (1), a court concludes that evidence was obtained in a manner that infringed or denied any rights or freedoms guaranteed by this Charter, the evidence shall be excluded if it is established that, having regard to all the circumstances, the admission of it in the proceedings would bring the administration of justice into disrepute.[24]

Confession Rule for Young Offenders – Section 146 Youth Criminal Justice Act

146. (1) Subject to this section, the law relating to the admissibility of statements made by persons accused of committing offences applies in respect of young persons.

(2) No oral or written statement made by a young person who is less than eighteen years old, to a peace officer or to any other person who is, in law, a person in authority, on the arrest or detention of the young person or in circumstances where the peace officer or other person has reasonable grounds for believing that the young person has committed an offence is admissible against the young person unless:

> (a) the statement was voluntary;
>
> (b) the person to whom the statement was made has, before the statement was made, clearly explained to the young person, in language appropriate to his or her age and understanding, that

(i) the young person is under no obligation to make a statement,

(ii) any statement made by the young person may be used as evidence in proceedings against him or her,

(iii) the young person has the right to consult counsel and a parent or other person in accordance with paragraph (c), and

(iv) any statement made by the young person is required to be made in the presence of counsel and any other person consulted in accordance with paragraph (c), if any, unless the young person desires otherwise;

> (c) the young person has, before the statement was made, been given a reasonable opportunity to consult

(i) with counsel, and

(ii) with a parent or, in the absence of a parent, an adult relative or, in the absence of a parent and an adult relative, any other appropriate adult chosen by the young person, as long as that person is not a co-accused, or under investigation, in respect of the same offence; and

> (d) if the young person consults a person in accordance with paragraph (c), the young person has been given a reasonable opportunity to make the statement in the presence of that person.
>
> (3) The requirements set out in paragraphs (2)(b) to (d) do not apply in respect of oral statements if they are made spontaneously by the young person to a peace officer or other person in authority before that person has had a reasonable opportunity to comply with those requirements.
>
> (4) A young person may waive the rights under paragraph (2)(c) or (d) but any such waiver
>
> (a) must be recorded on video tape or audio tape; or
>
> (b) must be in writing and contain a statement signed by the young person that he or she has been informed of the right being waived.

---

24   July 15, 2006 from: http://www.canlii.ca/ca/com/chart/s-24-2.html

(5) When a waiver of rights under paragraph (2)(c) or (d) is not made in accordance with subsection (4) owing to a technical irregularity, the youth justice court may determine that the waiver is valid if it is satisfied that the young person was informed of his or her rights, and voluntarily waived them.

(6) When there has been a technical irregularity in complying with paragraphs (2)(b) to (d), the youth justice court may admit into evidence a statement referred to in subsection (2), if satisfied that the admission of the statement would not bring into disrepute the principle that young persons are entitled to enhanced procedural protection to ensure that they are treated fairly and their rights are protected.

(7) A youth justice court judge may rule inadmissible in any proceedings under this Act a statement made by the young person in respect of whom the proceedings are taken if the young person satisfies the judge that the statement was made under duress imposed by any person who is not, in law, a person in authority.

(8) A youth justice court judge may in any proceedings under this Act rule admissible any statement or waiver by a young person if, at the time of the making of the statement or waiver,

(a) the young person held himself or herself to be eighteen years old or older;

(b) the person to whom the statement or waiver was made conducted reasonable inquiries as to the age of the young person and had reasonable grounds for believing that the young person was eighteen years old or older; and

(c) in all other circumstances the statement or waiver would otherwise be admissible.

(9) For the purpose of this section, a person consulted under paragraph (2)(c) is, in the absence of evidence to the contrary, deemed not to be a person in authority.

∞

Basic Translation – The Focus

The Confessions Rule and section 24(2) Charter are the nucleus of an endless network of case law decisions that interpret and translate both rules. Both rules are abstract concepts; case law turns them to concrete. For example, case law explains what exactly constitutes voluntary and reliable and how to achieve both concepts. Case law explains the decision-making process that governs how sec. 24 (2) Charter is applied. The two basic rules of evidence and the case law that flows from them, form a growing network of laws and strategies that, when viewed as a whole, seems overwhelmingly complicated for three reasons:

i.   There are two separate paths of rules that must intersect and fit together using a specific communication strategy.

ii. Both paths are always under construction. They're works-in-progress, perpetually evolving and being shaped by case law decisions that continuously add and subtract by defining, re-defining, interpreting, and translating.

iii. They are written in non-functional, impractical language. Much of statue and case law language is written in academic-speak instead of practical, usable language that can be functionally applied on the frontlines of law enforcement.

Despite the complexities, the basic idea is relatively simple – don't lose focus of the two fundamental characteristics of a confession, to a PIA, for guaranteed admissibility:

i.   illegal inducement-free, and;

ii. Charter violation-free.

Build a communication style based on a prevention plan/promotion plan that integrates both basic rules to prevent illegal inducements and prevent Charter violations while promoting legal inducements and promoting the instruction and delivery of Charter rights. The key is to become both a content expert and a communications expert. Integrating the language of both rules is the only way to prevent what excludes while promoting what admits – dual meaning. Promote what will convince the suspect to truthfully admit to the crime and promote the process that gets the admissions admitted as evidence at the trial. Maintain this logic – don't force a person to confess, don't force a suspect to say or adopt anything that isn't 100% true. Resist the temptation to short-circuit the offender's Charter rights. Start with perspective – Charter rights don't work against the police.

I was a uniform officer in 1982 when the Charter was enacted. Two years later, I was a detective. Initially, I was conditioned to fear the Charter, to view it as an unfair obstacle that blocked my job. Then I woke up. Experience changed my perspective. Preventing Charter violations is simple. There's nothing difficult about it. Some offenders called their lawyers, some waived their right. Some offenders confessed after they consulted with lawyers, some didn't. Some offenders confessed after they waived their right to counsel, some didn't. I opened my eyes… every case depended on the relationship between four factors: what I said, how I said it, what the offender believed, what the offender didn't believe. What the offender believes is the X-Factor and determines whether s/he confesses or not. An offender's beliefs are developed over a lifetime. A specific level of moral belief about what is right and wrong has to be reached to activate the guilty person's inner compulsion to confess. I learned that what I said and how I said it directly influenced whether the inner switch was flipped.

I learned that the interrogator controls whether a true confession is obtained or not and whether it's admitted or thrown out. I learned there's no one to blame but myself if I fail. If a confession was thrown out, I learned that **I** threw it out by fucking it up. I learned that interrogation is no different from any other job I've had… there are rules that have to be followed if you want to score points. I learned that interrogation rules are hard to learn and put in play but every profession has rules, some just as hard to learn and put into play. I learned that it wasn't as difficult as I thought to instruct an arrested person about Charter rights. In fact, it's easy. It's not quantum physics, it's not brain surgery. There's nothing difficult about removing illegal inducements from your language and conduct. It's simple to stick to the language of legal, moral inducements if you practice building a communication style that makes the right impact instead of the wrong one.

The "Twin Goals" – Striking the Balance

The main reason for failed interrogation is broken focus. Losing focus loses sight of where you're going. If the investigation *focus* is lost, it is easy to see only the complexity instead of the simplicity. *Don't ignore simplicity* – it is the main concept that forms and maintains the investigative focus. The starting point of making the focus second nature is by always remembering the "twin goals" of the Criminal Justice System (CJS) – protect the rights of the accused, protect society. Strike the balance by "protecting the rights of the accused without unduly limiting society's needs to investigate and solve crimes."[25]

The CJS twin goals represent common-sense objectives – fairness and neutrality. The CJS wants crimes solved without favouring or hindering either side: the public or the offender. The admissibility of confession is not supposed to be unattainable or unreasonably difficult. It's not supposed to be unreachable or unreasonable.

25   R. v. Oickle (2000), File No. 26535 (S.C.C.).

The rules are intended to strike the balance without putting the public or the offender at risk. The Rules of Evidence are not intended to work against anyone. They are intended to work for *everyone* to achieve the "twin goals" and *strike the balance* that protects both society and the offender's rights. That's the investigative focus. Keeping the twin goals in mind ensures clarity of purpose – you'll see the point of every rule, every law, every procedure, and every strategy. Clarity of purpose is the basic essential of consciousness-raising that lifts you to the next level of investigative expertise. If you lose sight of purpose, you'll see only what you want to see and not see what you don't what to see.

The CJS "Overriding Concern"

The CJS has an "overriding concern" in the pursuit of the "twin goals" – *not to convict innocent people*.[26] The prevention of wrongful conviction is the highest CJS priority. Charging an innocent person is a travesty. Convicting an innocent person is a cardinal sin that stains society.

If you work in law enforcement, you likely have been the victim of lies. Being the target of lies is part of the law enforcement job description. The science of "covering your ass" goes beyond empty words. It's real, it's a real-life survival skill. You have to become an expert at it or real-life will eat you up. False accusations made by arrested persons caused me to build professional paranoia throughout my police career. I've never forgotten the feeling of being the victim of outright lies. Allegations made by arrested people for the purpose of bargaining – using their false allegations as bargaining tool to help them escape out of their predicament. Many people suggest dropping the bad parts of one's past. I prefer to keep them. Keeping the bad memories on speed dial prevents history from repeating itself and prevents you from repeating history. The CJS "overriding concern" became a sticking point for me during my police career and it stuck with me after I resigned and changed careers. It became my primary concern when I taught law enforcement in college. It became my primary concern when I started writing law enforcement textbooks. Hate is a strong word. I hated being lied about. I always want to prevent it from happening to anyone else.

The "overriding concern" is the reason why tainted confessions are strictly prohibited from admission at trial. Any reasonable doubt about voluntariness of a confession to the police logically excludes the confession. This is one of the safeguards in place that create an *accountability* system wherein the prosecution has a strong burden of proof and a high standard to reach to *justify* the admissibility of a confession to a PIA. The need for the highest level of accountability is obvious but it sometimes can cross the line by creating an air of suspicion. The high level of accountability comes with a price. It often causes an environment of excessive negativity and suspicion about interrogations, confessions, and police motives. As difficult as it may be to work under a powerful microscope, learn to live with it. Learn to work with it. Learn to thrive on it instead of letting intense scrutiny piss you off. Use it to your advantage by becoming a professional survivor. Professionally covering your ass makes you an expert faster than any classroom work can teach you. Never back away from intense scrutiny. It's your strongest ally. When you can prove over and over again that you have played the game strictly according to the rules, no lies about you can ever win. The harder the test, the better the opportunity to score high marks. When you pass the highest test levels, your credibility soars.

Embed the "overriding concern" into your consciousness. Show it, straight from your heart. No matter how bad you want to solve a crime, no matter how hard you have to cover your ass, always show it – show your legitimate concern for the "overriding concern." Show your highest concern for preventing the worst nightmare – falsely accusing an innocent person. The false allegation is just as bad as a false conviction. The moment a person is falsely accused, his/her life becomes hell. False allegations are inexcusable. It's the worst form of professional bullying imaginable.

---

26   Ibid.

Chapter 5
History of the Confessions Rule

What "was" determines what is and what will be. History lessons are essential. They're not space-fillers. The history of the Confessions Rule is essential because every step of the evolution is a key lesson in fully understanding the current Contemporary Confessions Rule.

The original/traditional Confessions Rule, created by common law a century ago, defined voluntary by one simple element – a confession free from inducement. The absence of inducement was the only element that composed the concept of voluntary, constituting a *narrow* definition. During the next 86 years until *R. v. Oickle (2000)*, a chain of major events occurred including three landmark cases that added 3 additional factors to the concept of voluntary: (i) oppression, (ii) operating mind, and (iii) trickery. Additionally, a major legislative enactment (Charter) occurred and a body of academic research emerged revealing the growing problem of false confessions.

The following is a case law evolution of the Confessionsrule and the concept of "voluntariness."

In 1914, the original Confessions Rule was created in England in the landmark case, *Ibrahim v. The King*.[27] The *Ibrahim* rule, also called the "Traditional Confessions Rule," introduced the concept of voluntary, prohibited automatic admissibility of a confession made to a PIA, while imposing the onus on the prosecution to prove voluntariness. The *Ibrahim* rule was the product of a five-century evolution of self-incrimination laws relating to both trials and investigations. Since the sixteenth century, self-incrimination laws had been controversial and inconsistent. The *Ibrahim* rule was a solution. It solved the self-incrimination controversy and became the *common law* origin of the Canadian Confessions Rule.

The *Ibrahim* rule defined voluntary as the absence of "fear of prejudice" or "hope of advantage" exercised or held out by a PIA.[28] It protected an accused person from being tortured or coerced into confession, by threats or promises, held out by someone whom the accused reasonably believed was a PIA. Consequently, the original concept of voluntary had a narrow/single-element definition.[29]

In 1922 the *Ibrahim* rule was adopted in Canada by the S.C.C. in *Prosko v. The King (1922)*,[30] and in 1949 it was applied by the S.C.C. in *Boudreau v. The King (1949)*.[31] This case included 3 elements:

i. The *Ibrahim* rule was confirmed.

ii. The rule applied only to inculpatory statements (exculpatory statements were not included).

iii. "Voluntary" was defined as *"free from inducements* of persons in authority" which not only defined voluntary as meaning no inducement, it suggested a stricter approach of minimal tolerance for any type or any degree of inducement.

In 1978, the S.C.C., in *Erven v. The Queen (1978)*,[32] expanded the *Ibrahim* rule to include 2 types of statements: (i) inculpatory, and (ii) exculpatory, and, three time periods: (i) before, (ii) during, and (iii) after the crime.

---

27   Ibrahim v. The King (1914) 24 Cox C.C. 174.
28   R. v. Oickle (2000), File No. 26535 (S.C.C.).
29   Ibid.
30   Prosko v. The King (1922), 38 C.C.C. 199 (S.C.C.); R. v. Oickle (2000), File No. 26535 (S.C.C.).
31   Boudreau v The King (1949), 94 C.C.C. 1 (S.C.C.).
32   Erven v. The Queen (1978), 44 C.C.C. (2d) 76 (S.C.C.); R. v. Oickle (2000), File No. 26535 (S.C.C.).

The "operating mind" doctrine was added to the concept of "voluntary" in 1979 by the S.C.C. in *R. v. Ward* (1979)[33], *R. v. Howath* (1999)[34], and later in *R. v. Whittle* (1994).[35]

In 1981, the issue of "police trickery" was added to the concept of voluntariness by the S.C.C. in *R. v. Rothman* (1981),[36] and in 1982 the "atmosphere of oppression" was added by the S.C.C. in *R. v. Hobbins.*[37]

1982 saw the enactment of The Canadian Charter of Rights and Freedoms (The Charter). It created the second admissibility rule, sec. 24(2) which did not affect the concept of voluntary but made a separate rule.

Finally, in 2000, in the landmark case, *R. v. Oickle,*[38] the S.C.C.:

i.   recognized the growing body of research and academic literature that demonstrated not only the problem of false confession but that there are five basic kinds of false confessions and accompanying causes;

ii. reviewed the 86-year case law continuum for the purpose of identifying a need to modify the Traditional Confessions Rule; and

iii. made four major modifications to the original Traditional Confessions Rule:

    a.   the concept of "reliability" was added to the concept of "voluntary",

    b.   "Quid pro quo" was added to the definition of "inducement",

    c.   four elements were listed as factors that define and determine voluntariness and reliability: (i) inducements, (ii) oppression, (iii) operating mind, and (iv) police trickery.

    d.   "voluntary" has to be determined <u>contextually</u>. This means that the four elements (c.) have to be evaluated within the *context* of the entire interrogation. This represented a shift to a common-sense, flexible approach. This flexibility added common-sense investigative leeway because it loosened the strict exclusion of a confession that emerges following a minor/weak inducement (Part 2 of this book is devoted to a thorough explanation of Oickle).

2001 to the present represents a period of time called "The *Oickle* Derivatives." The *Oickle* decision has been applied in countless cases, shaping the principles created in *Oickle* in 2000. The derivative case law are concrete examples of how the Contemporary Confessions Rule works. Subsequent chapters are devoted to some of those case law decisions to demonstrate what interrogation strategies are acceptable and those that are unacceptable.

33   R. v. Ward (1979) 2 S.CR 30 (S.C.C.).
34   R. v. Howath (1979) 2 S.CR 376 (S.C.C.).
35   R. v. Whittle (1994) 2 S.CR 914 (S.C.C.).
36   R. v. Rothman (1981) 1 S.CR 640 (S.C.C.).
37   R. v. Hobbins (1982(1 S.CR 553 (S.C.C.).
38   R. v. Oickle (2000), File No. 26535 (S.C.C.).

Chapter 6
Evidentiary Strength of a Confession – Forming Reasonable Grounds

Confessions are not created equal. Each confession has a purpose but its evidentiary strength varies by value and significance. The strength of a confession is connected to belief – what it makes you believe during an investigation; what it makes the judge/jury believe during a trial. Belief is connected to justification. What is believed justifies specific actions and outcomes. Level of belief gives direction. Level of belief is the key in the investigation and prosecution of cases, and all levels of belief are connected to strength of evidence. How strong your evidence is determines how strong you believe. How strong you believe determines what you can do – direction.

The whole point of a true confession is to make you and others believe, leaving no doubt that you have not arrested or charged an innocent person. Erasing doubt is essential. "Reasonable grounds" is the level of belief that acts as the investigative objective, that target of belief that you aim for during an investigation. "Reasonable grounds" is the litmus test that justifies charging, arresting, and searching. The CJS is predicated on the concept of "belief," referring to a level of certainty about guilt, i.e., a specific person's connection to a specific crime. Strength of belief is tied to outcome – the stronger the belief the greater the outcome. **The key point is that a true confession made to any credible person (citizen or police) represents the strongest level of belief.**

There are four levels of belief, based on strength of certainty: one maximum level and three minimum standards. All three minimum standards of belief fall short of 100% certainty – each one has some extent of doubt – but represent a prosecutorial or investigative *goal*.

The maximum level of belief is 100% absolute certainty – no doubt. The three minimum standards of belief are:

i. Beyond a reasonable doubt (BRD), the belief standard for a prima facie case (conviction).

ii. Reasonable grounds (RG), an investigative standard for arresting, searching, and laying a charge.

iii. Mere suspicion (MS), the standard for investigative detention.

Quantity and quality of evidence is directly related to belief; belief is the by-product of evidence analysis. In other words, a belief is the outcome of decision-making made by analyzing evidence. The belief-forming/ decision-making process occurs twice – first during the investigation, secondly during the trial. Beliefs are not always static; they are fluctuating concepts, subject to change. Belief-forming occurs during the development of a narrative that evolves with the accumulation of evidence. During the *narrative* development, a belief may strengthen or weaken. The final belief is made at the conclusion of the narrative after all evidence is evaluated for credibility and strength.

The investigative/prosecution goal is to strengthen belief – create the maximum level of certainty or guilt. The defense goal is to *diminish* belief – raise at least a reasonable doubt. The best way to strengthen belief and remove all doubt is a true confession to any credible person – police or citizen. But neither the Confessions Rule nor sec. 24(2) Charter explain the evidentiary strength of a confession. Neither rule explains exactly what level of belief a confession constitutes. Does a confession alone form RG? Does a confession alone prove guilt BRD? To answer these questions, the following 12 points relating to the evidentiary strength and value of confessions must be understood:

1. There are two types of recipients of confessions, two groups of people who are "receivers" of a confession:

    a. person in authority (PIA)

    b. person not in authority (PNIA)

Generally, citizens are PNIA; police officers are PIA. The receiver of a confession has to fall in one of those two categories. There is no other classification of "receiver."

2. A true confession to any person (citizen or police) represents the strongest level of belief – 100% absolute certainty.

3. During an **investigation**, any confession (verbal or written) made to any person (citizen or police) constitutes RG.

4. During a **trial**, an admissible true confession to any person, whether alone or in conjunction with other evidence, constitutes a prima facie case. This means that an admissible true confession constitutes a belief BRD. An admissible confession, to any person, achieves absolute certainty (no doubt exists).

5. The rules of confession admissibility are different for PIA and PNIA. A confession made to a PIA is *not* automatically admissible. A confession to a PNIA is automatically admissible.

6. A confession to a police officer must be proved to be **voluntary**. The prosecution has the onus to prove *voluntariness*. A voir dire is needed to prove the confession was voluntarily made.

7. The "voluntary" concept does not apply to a confession made to a citizen – neither the Confessions Rule nor sec. 24(2) applies to a confession made to a PNIA. In other words, the prosecution does not have the onus to prove the confession was voluntarily made – no voir dire is needed. However, the PNIA (citizen) must appear in court and testify. The testimony must be deemed credible. Conversely, a confession to a citizen has no value if the citizen fails to appear, or, does appear but is deemed to have weak or no credibility.

8. The recipient of a confession (whether citizen or police) is a witness. This means that s/he is included on the Crown "witness list." A subpoena will be issued to compel that person's appearance in court. Despite the fact that s/he is not an eyewitness, the recipient is called a "Crown witness," and is subject to credibility evaluations both during the investigation and later at the trial in order for RG to be formed and a belief BRD be reached.

9. Typically, Crown witnesses must testify – hearsay is generally inadmissible. The police generally cannot testify on the witness's behalf. Every recipient of a confession, by virtue of having to testify, is subject to cross-examination where the defence goal is to diminish credibility.

10. In the case of multiple offenders for one offence, a confession by one accomplice that implicates another accomplice represents:

    a. A confession that incriminates the offender who made it, and,

    b. RG to believe the accomplice participated in the offence.

     i. This means the offender who confessed will be a Crown witness in the accomplice's trial.

     ii. The offender who confessed is both an accused person and a witness.

     iii. The confession is a dual-purpose statement; it's both a confession and a witness statement.

11. Accomplice testimony does not require corroboration by law; supporting evidence is not mandatory. During an investigation, his/her testimony constitutes RG. If the accomplice appears, and is deemed credible, his evidence constitutes a prima facie case.

12. An inculpatory statement that is not a full confession *may* constitute RG, either alone or in conjunction with other evidence. The level of belief depends on the extent and strength of the inculpatory statement. To reach the reasonable grounds standard, an inculpatory/partial confession must lead to only *one logical conclusion* – the accused's guilt. The operative/key word is "logical." If multiple logical conclusions exist, an inculpatory statement constitutes only mere suspicion.

∞

Classifying a "Receiver" of a Confession as a PIA or a PNIA

Classifying the recipient as PIA (person in authority) or PNIA (person not in authority) determines which admissibility path the confession takes – with a voir dire or without a voir dire. The definitions for both PIA and PNIA are found in case law. The two most relevant are the Supreme Court of Canada decisions, *R. v. Grandinette* (2005)[39] and *R. v. Hodgson* (1998)[40] The following guidelines can be used to classify PIA and PNIA.

Only three groups of people absolutely fall under one list without exception: peace officers, prison guards, and prosecutors who are readily identifiable to the accused person are PIA. If an accused **knows** he is speaking with a police officer, correctional worker, or Crown Attorney, the recipient is automatically classified as a PIA (no exceptions). The key is the accused's knowledge.

Other than these three groups of people, there are no other **absolute** classifications. All other classifications are *probable* or *likely* but are transferable from one classification list to another. Consequently, only *general* classification lists can be composed.

The PNIA classification list includes any person who is *not* a readily identifiable police officer, prison guard, or prosecutor. Examples include, but are not limited to:

- Parent
- Teacher
- Doctor
- Clergy
- Employer

---

39   R. v. Grandinette (2005) 1 S.CR 27, 2005 (S.C.C.) 5 Docket #30096.
40   R. v. Hodgson (1998) 2 S.CR 449 (S.C.C.).

Generally, when an accused person confesses to any one on this list, the recipient is a PNIA. The confession is automatically admissible; *no* voir dire is needed to determine if the confession was voluntary. The confidentiality of the conversation may be protected for other reasons but generally not for criminal investigations and criminal trials.

Anyone on the PNIA list is *probably* a PNIA and is *capable* of becoming a PIA. In other words, it is possible for any PNIA to be re-classified as a PIA. The determining factor is the accused's reasonable *belief* about the person's legal status and ability to influence and control proceedings. If the accused *reasonably* believed he confessed to a *state agent,* the recipient is reclassified from PNIA to PIA.

The key elements of re-classification are the *reasonableness* of the accused's belief and the concept of influencing/ controlling the proceedings. A reasonable belief requires concrete evidence as justification. It does not include a simple cursory statement that, "I believed he could control proceedings."

The concept of influencing and controlling the proceedings refers to a state agent role in either the:

    i.   investigation of a crime, or

    ii. apprehension of the offender, or

    iii. starting the proceedings (laying the Information), or

    iv. prosecution, including the discretion to withdraw an Information (drop a charge), or;

    v. working in collaboration with the police/prosecution team.

Usually, complainants/victims/witnesses have authority to do the third ("iii" above) task only – any person is authorized by the Criminal Code to lay an Information. However, they are not generally involved in the other roles. Usually, their participation in the proceedings is compelled by subpoena. State agents are characterized by extensive legal discretion – choice, decisions. Subpoenas remove discretion – they compel court attendance and participation. Collaboration with the police/prosecution team requires direction, instruction, or supervision by the police/prosecution team.

Consequently, re-classification of PNIA to PIA requires an accused's reasonable, justified belief that the PNIA was acting on behalf of the state through a formal partnership or arrangement. The PNIA must be an extension of the police/prosecution team in order to be re-classified as a PIA. Undercover police officers are generally PNIA.

The status *alone* of parents, teachers, doctors, and employers does not constitute a reasonable belief of the state agent role. Neither does the mere fact that a PNIA has some extent of authority over the accused. The re-classification depends on the extent of authority as an agent of the police/prosecution team.

The re-classification of PNIA to PIA requires a 3-step process:

Step 1: Offender/defence application.

Step 2: Offender/defence onus to "demonstrate that there is a *valid issue* for consideration."

Step 3: If step #2 is successful, then the Crown has the onus to prove beyond a reasonable doubt, that the recipient was a PNIA.

This 3-step process is conducted during a voir dire – a hearing to determine the classification of the "receiver." The defence must initiate the voir dire by applying and then has the first burden of proof – a comparatively low standard of proof that reclassification is a valid issue. If proven, the voir dire onus shifts to the Crown to prove beyond a reasonable doubt that the recipient was a PNIA.

There is one exception to the requirement for the defence initiating the voir dire by applying for it. In rare cases, a trial judge may have the *duty* to initiate a reclassification voir dire when evidence introduced during the trial reveals a "realistic" need for the hearing.

PIA/PNIA Classification Lists

PIA List Absolute	PNIA List Generally
Peace Officer	Complainant/Victim
Prison Guard	Accused's Parent
Prosecutor	Accused's Relative
PNIA, if proved to be an agent of police/prosecution and if offender has knowledge	Under-cover police officer
	Doctor/Psychiatrist
	Clergy
	Non-state agent
	Teacher

Investigative Goal: The Strategic Model

There are three investigative strategies connected to a confession made to a PNIA:

1. Communication Transfer Theory: The Communication Transfer Theory is like the Transfer/Exchange Theory of physical evidence that teaches it's impossible to commit a crime without physical evidence being transferred. Physical evidence will be exchanged in every crime – from person-to-person, item-to-item, or item-to-person. I believe the same applies to communication. I believe that no offender can remain silent forever about a crime. The worse the crime, the more likely and sooner it will happen. The reason is the pressure of cognitive dissonance. The inner hell of guilt over the crime has to be relieved by confession to someone. The offender leaves a trail of communication just like a trail of physical evidence. The key is finding it.

2. When you take a statement from a citizen who is the recipient of a confession from a suspect, include the entire context – what was said and done, before, during, and after the confession. This will prove the suspect's state of mind about the receiver's ability to influence the prosecution of the case.

3. If you question a suspect in the presence of a citizen, rule #2 applies – note the context. A citizen in your presence is a receiver of a confession but your presence may classify that citizen as a PIA. If a citizen is re-classified as a PIA, be prepared for a void dire.

A confession may represent the entirety of the Crown's case or part of it. Every case has main evidence – the centerpiece or focal point. Arguably, a confession is always the main evidence because its value supersedes all other types of evidence. However, when a victim or eyewitness' observations exist, a confession is often considered corroboration (supporting evidence) to the main evidence represented by a witness or physical evidence. Regardless, there is no such thing as a case that is strong enough without a confession. There is no case where the amount of evidence can be considered so overwhelming that a confession isn't needed. There is no such thing as an air-tight case where a confession would not benefit or strengthen the Crown's case. It doesn't matter how much physical evidence exists or how many eye-witnesses exist. A confession can always benefit or strengthen a case no matter how solid the case is. Here's a simple investigative principle to ingrain into your philosophy: Always interrogate every arrested person. Always try to obtain a confession regardless of how many witnesses or how much physical evidence exists. The reasons are:

1. Witness credibility is always a potential problem.

2. Witness failure to appear is always a potential problem.

3. A witness changing his/her story is always a potential problem.

4. Physical evidence, regardless of how strong it may incriminate the suspect, may be tainted by credibility issues of the witnesses who have to introduce the evidence. Physical evidence is only as strong as the credibility of the witness who has to introduce it. The strength of physical evidence is directly connected to the credibility of continuity and the humans responsible for it.

5. A confession has the strongest value of any evidence – it makes sense to try to get a confession in each case.

6. The offender may confess to other crimes.

7. The offender may provide information implicating other offenders.

Every suspect may have committed a number of unsolved crimes. Every suspect may know who has committed unsolved crimes. A suspect is the equivalent of a crime scene – s/he is a valuable source of potential evidence. One suspect can solve more crime faster than any other investigative strategy and with less expense.

Editorial: I will repeat the following 3-step investigative philosophy throughout this book:

> Step 1. Get a true confession for the original crime – the one being investigated.
>
> Step 2. Get true confessions for every unsolved crime the suspect has committed in his/her entire life.
>
> Step 3. Get statements about confessions s/he has received from other offenders, and/or eyewitness statements about observations that implicate other offenders (for as many unsolved crimes as possible).

An interrogation is a *proactive strategy* that may solve multiple crimes in the shortest time. It's an efficient way to protect the public from career offenders who go on crime sprees and become fully immersed in the criminal culture. Additionally, as the Supreme Court of Canada stated, cleaning the slate is way for the offender to rehabilitate and reintegrate.

Summary: The Admissibility Objective

The "admissibility objective" refers to the investigative goals created by the two pathways of rules of evidence: the Confessions Rule and Section 24(2) Charter. The following summary emphasizes the key points that must be understood before moving on to an explanation of *Oickle* and *Grant*.

Key Point #1: The Confessions Rule creates the "voluntary/reliable" rule. Section 24(2) Charter creates the "no Charter violation" rule. Consequently, the admissibility objective is an equation represented by the dual goals: voluntary + no Charter violation = admissible confession.

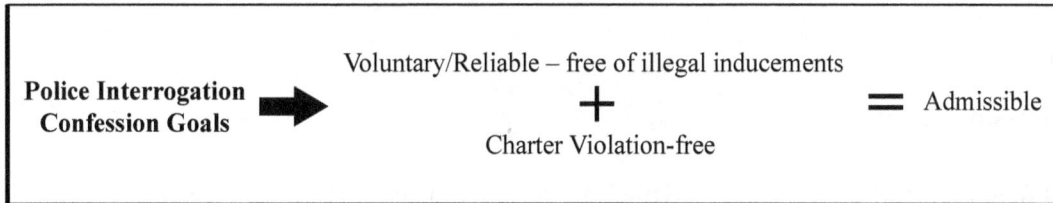

Key Point #2: The purpose of the two pathways of rules is to *protect* the person being questioned from being *forced* to confess and from being denied his/her Charter rights. Simultaneously, neither set of rules are supposed to unreasonably restrict the investigation of crime.[41] They create the boundaries but not the specific practices. Additionally, each set of rules has two types of meanings: limitless – meaning more specific, concrete interpretation, complex; emerging from countless case law; and, base – meaning general, abstract or simple.

The Base Meaning

The base meaning for the two rules is as follows:

Confessions Rule	Section 24(2) Charter
Traditional: Any statement made by an offender to a PIA, before, during, or after an offence is admissible *if* the prosecution proves the statement was voluntarily made.	Any evidence obtained after the commission of a Charter violation *may* be admissible *if* the admission of the evidence will not bring the administration of justice into disrepute.[43]
Contemporary: A statement made by an offender to a PIA, before, during, or after a crime is admissible if the prosecutor proves that the statement was *voluntary* and *reliable*, within the *context* of the circumstances, considering four factors: threats or promises, oppression, operating mind, and trickery.[42]	

---

41   R. v. Oickle (2000), File No. 26535 (S.C.C.).
42   Ibid.
43   Sec. 24(2) Charter.

Key Point #3: The Confessions Rule is separate from the Charter and has nothing to do with Charter violations. The Confessions Rule is characterized by 7 elements that trigger its applicability:

1. What type of statement

2. Made by whom (originator)

3. To whom (recipient)

4. When

5. How

6. Onus

7. Admissibility

What type of statement: The Confessions Rule applies to both inculpatory and exculpatory statements. The reason is that a denial or alibi proved false becomes inculpatory.

Made by whom: The originator must be a suspect or accused person. In other words, the Confessions Rule applies to *offenders*, not witnesses.

To whom: The recipient must be a PIA. If the recipient is a person *not* in authority, the Confessions Rule does not apply. This means a statement by an offender to a person *not* in authority is *automatically admissible.*

When: There are 3 time periods when an offender may make the statement – before, during, and after the crime. The Confessions Rule applies to all three time periods.

How: Voluntary.

Onus: The prosecution has the onus to prove the statement was voluntarily made.

Admissibility: Conditional. A confession to a PIA is *not* automatically admissible. A voir dire (admissibility hearing) must be conducted *during* the trial, at which time, the prosecutor has the burden to prove that the accused person confessed voluntarily. If the prosecution succeeds, the confession is admissible. If the prosecution fails, the confession is considered *involuntary* and it will be excluded (it will be deemed inadmissible).

The following two concepts emerge from the 7 elements listed above.

1. A confession to a person NOT in authority requires *no voir dire*. The confession is automatically admissible. The Crown prosecutor has no onus to prove voluntary.

2. A voir dire is mandatory at a trial regarding a confession to person authority. A confession to the police is *not* automatically admissible. The Crown must introduce evidence (witness) during the vior dire to prove beyond a reasonable doubt that the offender confessed voluntarily. The accused is entitled to waive a voir dire. If he/she does, the voir dire technically occurred but the accused admitted he/she confessed voluntarily. Regardless, the *compulsory* voir dire rule applies to every confession made to the police.

Key Point #4: Section 24(2) Charter has nothing to do with voluntariness. Instead, it is the premier rule of admissibility that applies to all evidence, not only confessions. It applies to evidence that emerges from an offender, e.g., confession, breath sample, blood sample, and evidence that does not emerge from an offender, e.g., a physical item such as a weapon or drugs. This rule protects the offender's rights as guaranteed to him/her by sections 7-14 Charter. The same 7 elements apply:

1.   What type of statement

2.   Made by whom (originator)

3.   To whom (recipient)

4.   When

5.   How

6.   Onus

7.   Admissibility

What type of statement: Inculpatory or exculpatory (same as Confessions Rule).

Made by whom (originator): Suspect or accused person (same as Confessions Rule).

To whom (recipient): A *state agent*, referring to a person employed by or working on behalf of a level of government.[44] This definition includes the police but not private citizens. "State agent" has a similar meaning as PIA. This means the Charter does not apply to non-state agents. The sec 24(2) Charter rule does not apply to confessions made to non-state agents.

When: A sequence must occur for the rule to apply. A Charter violation must occur *first* followed by the confession. If this sequence does not occur or exist, the rule does not apply. In other words, a Charter violation is the starting point that mobilizes this rule.[45]

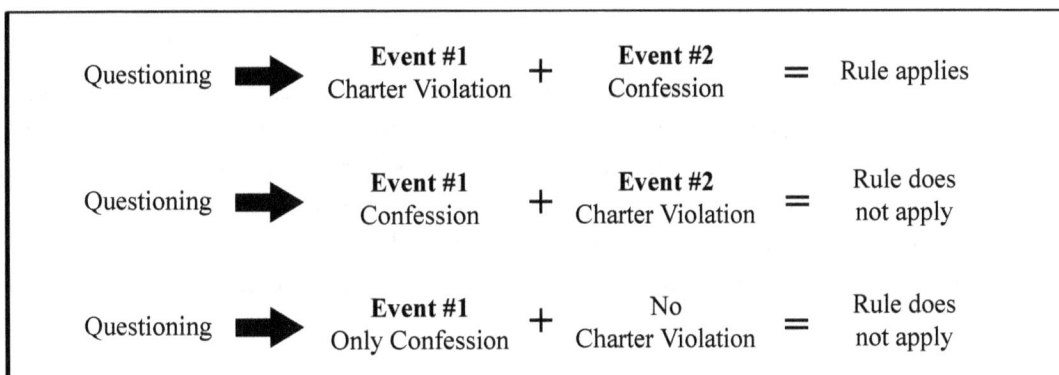

Questioning →	Event #1 Charter Violation	+	Event #2 Confession	=	Rule applies
Questioning →	Event #1 Confession	+	Event #2 Charter Violation	=	Rule does not apply
Questioning →	Event #1 Only Confession	+	No Charter Violation	=	Rule does not apply

---

44   Sec. 32 Charter.
45   R. v. Stillman (1997), 113 C.C.C. (3d) 321 (S.C.C.); R. v. Collins (1987), 33 C.C.C. (3d) 1 (S.C.C.).

How: The issue is the sequence – a confession must emerge from the Charter violation. "How" refers to the effect of the violation on the outcome, i.e., a confession.

Onus: Accused person. This is different from the Confessions Rule. The accused person has the burden to prove a Charter violation occurred and that it *preceded* the confession. Additionally, the standard of proof is different from the Confessions Rule. The accused only has to prove the violation occurred on a "balance of probabilities," a level below "beyond reasonable doubt."[46]

Admissibility: After the accused proves that a Charter violation *occurred* and *preceded* the confession, the trial judge must make a decision – admit or exclude the confession. The criteria is simple – the effect that the admission or exclusion of the confession will have on the reputation of the CJS. If admission of the confession negatively affects CJS reputation, the confession is inadmissible. The model for making this decision is found in *R. v. Grant* (2009). Prior to *Grant* the *Collins* test was used.

Key Point #5: The following concepts emerge from these 7 elements.

1. If *no* Charter violation preceded the confession, the sec. 24(2) Charter rule does not apply – the confession is admissible.

2. If a Charter violation occurs *after* a confession, the rule does not apply – the confession is admissible.

3. If a Charter violation occurs first, before a confession, the rule applies but the confession is *NOT automatically* excluded or admissible. A judge must decide based on the effect on the CJS reputation. In other words, a confession made *after* a Charter violation *may* be admissible.

Key Point #6: Comparison/Contrast – 2 Rules

There are eight points of comparison and contrast to help understand the two rules. Three points are the same. Both rules apply to:

i.   inculpatory or exculpatory statements,

ii. made by an accused person/suspect,

iii. to a person-in-authority.

The rules differ on five points. The Confessions Rule has a broader scope. It applies to before, during, and after the offence. The sec. 24(2) Charter rule applies to a more limited time period – usually upon arrest or detention. The onus to prove the violation and the standard of proof are different. The Crown has the onus to prove "voluntary beyond a reasonable doubt." The accused person has the onus to prove the commission of a Charter violation on the balance of probabilities (lower standard – less evidence). The nature/central focus of the violation is different. The Confessions Rule issue is voluntariness; the sec. 24(2) issue is a Charter violation.

Finally, the remedy after a violation is different. Remedy refers to the method of correcting the wrong. A Confessions Rule violation *must* exclude a confession (automatic/mandatory exclusion). A Charter violation *may* exclude a confession (not automatic, not compulsory – the Judge has discretion).

---

46   Ibid.

	Confessions Rule		Sec. 24 (2)Charter
Type of statement: inculpatory or exculpatory	Before, during or after crime ←	*When* →	Generally, upon arrest or detention
	Crown / prosecutor ←	*Onus* →	Accused / defense
Originator: accused/suspect	Beyond reasonable doubt ←	*Standard of proof* →	Balance of probabilities
Recipient: Police (PIA)	Voluntariness ←	*Central focus of violation* →	Charter violation
	Mandatory exclusion (automatically inadmissible) ←	*Remedy after violation* →	Possible exclusion (not automatically inadmissible)

Key Point #7: Recipient-voluntary Sequence

The Confessions Rule operates within a sequence of two control issues that form a two-step process:

Step #1: Is the recipient a PIA or PNIA?

Whether or not the Confessions Rule applies depends on the classification of the recipient and there are only two – PIA and PNIA. If the recipient is a PNIA, the Confessions Rule does not apply, the confession is automatically admissible and step #2 does not apply. If the recipient is a PIA, the Confessions Rule does apply, the confession is not automatically admissible, and step #2 is triggered.

Step #2: If the receiver is a PIA, is the confession voluntary?

The advantage of a confession to a person not in authority (PNIA) is automatic admissibility. No voir dire. The defence wants to prevent this by re-classifying as many PNIAs as *possible* PIAs to force the confession to undergo a voir dire (admissibility hearing).

Never underestimate the power of a confession to a PNIA. Usually it's an interrogation-free confession where the suspect voluntarily confesses without any prompting and without questioning. Finding confessions made to citizens doesn't absolve you of the obligation to get a confession but every confession you find that was made to someone other than a PIA is powerful corroboration that the confession made to you is true – voluntary and reliable.

Part II: *R. v. Oickle* (2000) S.C.C.

Part 1: Practical Translation

The point-of-reference case

Chapter 7
Circumstances of the case: The Interrogation

R. v. Oickle (2000) was a game-changer because it became the closest thing to an interrogation playbook that exists in Canadian law. It's the *point-of-reference* case that serves as the strategic centerpiece for all your interrogations; a general game plan that can be customized to any interrogation.

The original/traditional Confessions Rule, that emerged in common law in 1914, defined voluntary by one simple element – a confession free from inducement. The absence of inducement was the only element that composed the concept of voluntary, constituting a *narrow* definition. *Oickle* condensed the concepts that evolved during the 86 years from 1914-2000, including the growing body of academic research that brought attention to the problem of false confessions. *Oickle* is the solution to forced and/or false confessions by establishing: (i) how to prevent a false confession, (ii) how to get a true confession, and (iii) how to prove that the confession was truthful and voluntary.

The 2000 *Oickle* landmark decision by the S.C.C. modified the Confessions Rule and the concept of voluntary. The Court re-examined the original Confessions Rule and expanded it by adding to it a second concept of "reliability" – a response to the false confession research. The S.C.C. listed 4 factors that govern voluntariness and reliability. The first factor remained the *free from inducement* principle but the S.C.C. altered the definition to "no *improper* inducement." The other three elements added were the "oppression," "operating mind," and "trickery" elements. The circumstances of the interrogation in *Oickle* provide a model of legal, moral, concrete interrogation strategies. And it summarized conclusions that form both a theoretical and practical framework for interrogations.

Oickle isn't an investigative roadblock. It doesn't put obstacles in the way of interrogation. It removes them. *Oickle* opened up a path to preventing false confessions and silencing critics. It created an interrogation playbook approved by the Supreme Court of Canada. **Change your perspective, change the outcome.**

I've broken down *Oickle* into two parts. The first part of *Oickle* (this chapter) explains the actual case, the interrogation and the issues that were decided. The second part (next chapter) explains the Contemporary Confessions Rule and how it was made.

R. v. Oickle (2000) S.C.C.

Offences: Multiple counts of arson

Evidence: The police investigated a series of fires, involving buildings and vehicles, occurring over fourteen months. As a result of the investigation, the police made a list of eight suspects. Each was asked to submit to a polygraph test. The first six passed, narrowing the list. One of the two remaining suspects was initially reluctant to take the lie-detector test because of doubts about the test; he eventually consented. This suspect lived in close proximity to four of the building fires. One torched vehicle was owned by this person's fiancée and another one was owned by his father. All fires occurred between 1:00 and 4:00 a.m. Each fire was deliberately set. The accused was a volunteer firefighter who responded to each fire.

The accused's polygraph test was conducted with the accused's consent at 3 p.m. in a motel room. Although the accused was not under arrest at that time, he was informed of:

   i.   his right to silence,

   ii. his right to counsel,

   iii. his right to leave at any time,

   iv. the fact that the polygraph officer's interpretation of the polygraph results was not admissible but anything the accused said would be admissible.

A pamphlet explaining the polygraph procedure was given to the accused and he signed a consent form. The polygraph officer conducted a lengthy pre-test interview before conducting the test itself. It consisted of wide-ranging questions, including personal ones. The pre-test interview was designed to build trust and to compose control questions. At the conclusion, an exculpatory statement was taken, forming the basis of the polygraph test.

The actual polygraph test followed, lasting only a matter of minutes. The officer did not ask about any specific fire; instead, he asked only if the previous exculpatory statement was true. At the conclusion of the test and analysis, the officer informed the accused that he had failed the test, reminded him of his rights (although he wasn't under arrest), and questioned him for one hour. During this time, the accused asked, *"What if I admit to the car? Then I can walk out of here and it's over?"* The officer responded, *"You can walk out at any time,"* but the accused remained.

Another officer relieved the polygraph examiner. After 30 to 40 minutes, the accused confessed to setting fire to his fiancée's car. He was emotionally distraught, acknowledged his rights again, and gave a written confession to that offence only but denied the rest.

The accused was transported to the police station, three hours and 15 minutes after the test concluded. En route, he was still upset and crying. He was taken to an interview room with videotaping equipment that recorded the subsequent interrogation about the other fires. Twice he asked to go home to bed because he was tired. He was denied this request because he was under arrest. Questioning continued.

Another officer took over and questioned the accused for more than an hour. At 11:00 p.m., six hours after the polygraph test ended, the accused confessed to seven of the eight fires, denying he set fire to his father's van. The accused gave a written confession.

At 6:00 a.m., the accused consented to a re-enactment. The police drove him to each crime scene, where he described how he had set each fire.

At the trial, a voir dire was conducted regarding the confessions and the re-enactment. The trial judge ruled that they all were voluntary and admissible, resulting in convictions on all counts. The accused appealed to the Nova Scotia Court of Appeal. That court ruled that all statements were involuntary and were excluded, resulting in acquittals. The Crown appealed to the S.C.C. This court ruled that all statements were voluntary and admissible, thus restoring the convictions.

Issues: Nine common interrogation practices/strategies/issues were the central focus of the judgment. The S.C.C. ruled that each one was *not* an illegal inducement with the context of this specific interrogation. All nine were confirmed as legal, ethical interrogation practices/strategies, again, within the context of this specific interrogation.

The following is a list of the nine interrogation practices/strategies/issues:

1. Minimizing the severity of the crime.

2. Offers of psychiatric help.

3. "It would be better ..."

4. Using family as leverage – alleged threats against the accused's fiancée.

5. Building trust – the line between genuine trust and abuse of trust.

6. The absence of an atmosphere of oppression.

7. Failure to inform the suspect of the inadmissibility of polygraph test results.

8. Exaggerating the polygraph's validity.

9. Misleading the accused regarding the duration of the interview.

The following is a review of the judgment for all nine interrogation practices/strategies:

Strategy/issue #1

Minimizing the severity of the crime: The police used common interrogation strategies/practices intended to minimize the effect of multiple charges and to minimize the label of "criminal." At issue were three statements in particular made by the police:

i. *"There is little difference between being convicted of one fire compared to 10."*

ii. The multiple offences were considered to be a *"one package type of thing."*

iii. The officers said the accused was not really a criminal and that they did not want to treat him as one.

The S.C.C. ruled that none of these statements were illegal inducements. Although each statement did minimize the severity of the offence, they minimized the <u>moral significance</u> of the crimes, not the legal consequences. The police never suggested that a confession would minimize the legal consequences of the crimes. The following is the formal rule straight from the judgment:

> *"Minimizing the moral significance of an offence is a common and usually unobjectionable feature of police interrogation. The real concern is whether the police suggested that a confession will result in the <u>legal consequences being minimal.</u>"*

Translation: There's a clear part and a confusing part to this specific ruling. First the confusing part. The first two statements did discuss legal consequences and, on the surface, they did minimize the legal consequences. Packaging all counts into one for sentencing directly relates to legal consequences. But, the police were not lying. They were simply stating a fact. Sentencing is directed to the wrongdoing as a whole. Although multiple charges quantify wrongdoing, the legal perspective is that the entire context of all charges forms one contextual wrongdoing. The packaging of multiple charges is a moral issue, even though it appears to be a legal issue, on the surface. Morally, ten offences in one crime spree are considered one moral wrong. These types of "packaging" statements are common interrogation strategies because they are the truth. For the moral purpose of sentencing, it doesn't matter if the accused is charged with ten separate crimes or one. Both circumstances have the same moral consequence.

The clear part is that there's a big difference between the two concepts of moral consequence and legal consequence. Moral consequences can be minimized by the police during interrogation, legal consequences cannot; the legal consequences are off limits. You can't soften the legal blow. The best example of minimizing the legal consequences is offering a reduction in sentence in exchange for a confession. That constitutes an illegal inducement.

Telling the suspect that s/he is not a criminal, even though the CJS defines him/her as such, is not an illegal inducement. It's morally and legally acceptable to tell the suspect that negative labels, such as "criminal," won't be attached because of the crime. Reducing the impact of the crime on the suspect's reputation is a legal inducement and a permissible interrogation strategy to set the suspect's mind at ease about what label s/he will carry.

Here are practical lessons/key points for strategy #1:

1. Remove any reference of legal consequences from your vocabulary. Never use any statement to imply the minimizing of legal consequences. Don't suggest leniency or dramatic reduction in a sentence. Don't suggest the accused will "get off lightly" or "stay out of jail" or any other promise or hope of minimized legal consequences.

2. If the suspect asks you about the legal consequence, tell him/her exactly what the S.C.C. instructed – can't talk about it. Tell the truth. The S.C.C. ruled that the topic of legal consequences is off limits. Change the subject.

3. Moral consequences are not off limits. The S.C.C. gave only two examples in this ruling about what constitutes acceptable minimized moral consequences. The first is the concept of packaging crimes – one charge or ten, there's no difference. That's not an illegal inducement. Use it in cases when the suspect is facing multiple charges. Explain the rationale of that philosophy – rehabilitation and reintegrating are the objective along with protecting public safety. One charge or ten charges constitute the same level of moral wrong. Secondly, it's not an illegal inducement to remove the "criminal" label. Even though the suspect falls under the legal definition of "criminal," you can convince a suspect that morally he doesn't have to carry that burden. "Criminal" is a man-made label. It's part of the social condemnation process but not part of the spiritual condemnation process.

4. Moral consequences include spiritual consequences. It's not an illegal or unethical inducement to minimize the spiritual consequences by discussing the health and welfare of the suspect's soul and the suspect's relationship with God or the Higher Power that s/he believes in or doesn't believe in. The S.C.C. gave the green light to talk about spiritual forgiveness and spiritual healing. These are powerful topics that have the capacity to make a positive impact with any suspect. And it legally and ethically diverts the suspect's focus from the legal consequences which are a mountainous barrier to true confessions. The second example is minimizing the label, changing the label from criminal to otherwise.

5. Minimization of moral consequences is not a trick or gimmick or something to randomly throw into the interrogation. It's the opposite of using tactics and language that morally condemn. Moral condemnation doesn't achieve the top priority of appealing to the conscience. Moral condemnation and appealing to the conscience are two separate concepts. One doesn't work, the other does. Minimizing moral consequences is useless unless the words are spoken with authenticity. Words are empty and meaningless without sincerity and a compelling purpose to strike a chord. Like all humans, suspects have a bullshit detector, an inner radar that identifies disingenuousness. I could list pages of recommended statements (that constitute legal inducement) that can be used to minimize moral consequences but all are worthless if they are not spoken straight from the heart. There has to be some fire behind it. Fire doesn't mean wall-shaking fire and brimstone preaching. Fire is a word I use that means passion – passion for authenticity, passion for meaning what you're saying. Exceeding the dullness of a recorded message. In other words, minimizing moral consequences is a powerful motivator of the truth if the words are spoken with fire. Otherwise, empty words promote more emptiness.

Strategy/issue #2

Offers of psychiatric help: The police used a common phrase during this interrogation: *"I think you need help. Maybe you need professional help."* However, at no time did they suggest that this help would be received only in exchange for a confession. The S.C.C. ruled that the offer for psychiatric help was not an illegal inducement because the offer was not conditional on a confession.

Translation: Offering help is natural. It's natural for humans to offer help and to ask for help. All of us need help at some point. Sometimes we ask for help, sometimes we don't. But the world would be a mess if we couldn't offer help without being asked first. Committing crimes is a problem that needs a solution. Offering help is an act of problem-solving. There/s nothing wrong with offering help as long as it's not part of a deal; it's wrong only when there's a price tag – a confession. Conditional offers of any help, including psychiatric, in exchange for a confession are illegal inducements. Conversely, unconditional offers for help that are not dependent on a confession are legal inducements.

Practical lessons/Key points:

1. Don't use the word "help" by itself. Call it "professional help." Don't leave it up to the suspect to define "help" because s/he may believe you mean legal help – leniency, which constitutes an illegal inducement. Ingrain "professional help" into your vocabulary instead of just "help."

2. Professional help is a big step in anyone's life. Don't underestimate the gravity or the impact. The effect of suggesting professional help is not predictable with 100% certainty. It may work for or against you, depending on how the suspect takes it. The key is to discuss professional help as a solution to a problem, not the cause of more problems.

3. The topic of professional help has to lead to a successful conclusion – a solution to a problem that the suspect acknowledges. It needs a beginning and an end. Arbitrary calls for professional help are weak in comparison to a <u>message with purpose</u>. An offer for professional help is an exploration. It starts with a suggestion – either a direct suggestion by you or it can be the suspect's suggestion. *"You need help"* is one way to start but it could backfire if the suspect doesn't perceive it as a solution. *"Do you think you need professional help?"* is another angle. *"Have you ever thought of professional help?"* is one of the all-time best for several reasons: (i) it's not judgmental or confrontational, (ii) it shows

legitimate concern (iii) it diverts from the number-one hell in a suspect's mind – legal consequences (iv) if s/he answers "yes", you have made giant steps in establishing the unique type of rapport and trust needed to activate the suspect's compulsion to confess because the suspect just admitted an intimate detail of privacy – past personal thoughts. Divulging past thoughts of seeking professional help is deeply personal. It's one of the intangibles that contribute to activating the suspect's compulsion to confess. Never underestimate the power of such an admission.

4. If the answer is "yes", probe. Ask why he thought of seeking professional help. The reason is crucial. If he tells you, it's a major step toward a true confession. Let him spill his guts about the inner pain he's been suffering that led him to think about professional help. The inner pain is the biggest part of the suspect's problem. It's the cause of his criminal behaviour. Never cut him short. Never re-direct the conversation away from a suspect's narrative of his past. A suspect's past is the key to the present. Sharing what hurts inside is step for recovery and one of the final steps toward purging guilt.

5. Be a problem-solver, not a problem-causer. Crime prevention is the biggest part of crime-fighting. Solving the crime after the fact starts the process of preventing more of the same in the future. Focus on solutions for rehabilitation and reintegration. To achieve that, study the professional help that's available so you can discuss the matter with authority.

6. Be careful how you use statements such as, *"You have to help yourself."* Professional help is different from self-help. Professional help includes expert services and proven treatments intended to solve psychological problems. Self-help is reconciliation between self and conscience. Separate the two concepts. Don't mix them together. Confession is an inner change agent through reconciliation. Professional help is an external change agent. Be careful that "have to" isn't construed with being forced to confess for the sake of self-help.

7. Don't withhold help in exchange for a confession. Don't imply or suggest the need for professional help and then make it available only if you get a confession. Separate the dialogue with a clarifying statement: *"I want to talk to you about professional help. This has nothing to do with a confession."* The best way to ensure that no conditions are attached to an offer for professional help is to make a statement that clarifies the complete separation of professional help from a confession. Remember the word <u>instruction.</u> When you want the suspect to know something, instruct him. When you need to prove the suspect's knowledge about any key issue, instruct him. Teaching is an integral part of interrogation.

Strategy/issue #3

"It would be better ...": This interrogation included several police statements implying improvement. Specifically, the police suggested that a confession would, (i) make the suspect feel <u>better</u>, (ii) generate respect from his fiancée and members of the community, and (iii) <u>better</u> address his apparent pyromania.

The S.C.C. ruled that all of these statement amount to "moral inducements" which are legal. None of them were illegal inducements. The reason was that each statement lacked the element of implied threat or promise. Moral inducements appeal to the conscience to motivate a self-generated confession. Moral inducements are defined as "police statements that don't imply threats or promises." The following is a verbatim general rule by the S.C.C. straight from the judgment:

"Suggesting possible benefits of a confession is acceptable if no insinuation exists of an implied threat or promise."

Translation: Confessions are benefit-driven. Confessions don't just happen. They are driven by a need for a benefit, a desire to improve a negative. The suggestion of a benefit is a legal inducement as long as the benefit is not connected to a threat or promise relating to physical punishment or legal consequences. The S.C.C. encouraged the use of moral benefits to motivate a confession because they don't suggest or include threats or promises.

Practical lessons/Key points:

1. To be on the safe side, remove "better" from your vocabulary because the word "better" is abstract and open to wide-ranging interpretations including the threat of physical violence or the promise of leniency.

2. Be specific about the benefit. Use this case as an example: (i) feeling better – replace it with "finding peace", (ii) respect from family – state this benefit as: *"Your family will be proud",* (iii) psychological problems such as pyromania – can be stated as: *"You want to solve your problem of (insert psychological disorder or compulsion). Confessing is the first step."*

3. Never rely on only one statement about finding inner peace. The concept of "feeling better" has to be sold. The suspect has to buy-in. Depending on the strength of his conscience, buy-in will be easy or it will take work. Either way, start of by explaining the obvious:

    a. guilt causes pain,

    b. the pain of guilt will not go away on its own,

    c. the pain of guilt will get worse. It always does,

    d. the pain of guilt becomes chronic. It's a long-term ailment that will impair human functionality. It interferes with personal life and professional life. It's impossible to be happy and stress-free with chronic pain from guilt. Unresolved inner conflict progressively builds anxiety and spills out into the environment, and,

    e. the solution is confession. It all goes away by being honest and telling the truth. Keeping a secret locked inside will become crushing pain. Hiding the truth will never relieve the pain.

Strategy/issue #4

Using family as leverage: In this case, alleged threats against the accused's fiancée. The police told the accused that if he confessed, it would be unnecessary to subject his fiancée to extensive interrogation. The confession occurred two hours after the police made these remarks. The court ruled: (i) the timing showed *no connection* between the police inducement and the confession, (ii) their relationship had the required strength – it was strong enough to induce a false confession if she were in fact threatened. However, *no threat* was made toward her, and, (iii) the two elements of third-party inducement were not fulfilled.

The court ruled:

1. If the police had offered to drop pending charges against the fiancée or if they had threatened to charge her, the accused's confession would have been involuntary because of the inducements that would have existed.

2. Merely promising not to polygraph the fiancée in exchange for the confession was not a strong enough inducement to raise reasonable doubt about voluntariness.

Translation: Using a suspect's inner circle as leverage against the suspect is a slippery slope. It constitutes an illegal inducement if the police offer leniency, e.g., to withdraw charges against a loved one in exchange for a confession. This type of inducement has the capacity to cause a false confession. The mitigating factors are: (i) the strength of the emotional attachment, (ii) the type of offer, and, (iii) the impact of the offer.

The person being used as leverage has to be someone special in the suspect's life – "a loved one." The bond between the two has to be strong enough to force the suspect to do anything to save that person, including making up a confession. The offer has to have substance. The best example is leniency. A promise to drop charges is strong enough to generate a false confession. But a promise not to subject the loved one to investigation, including a polygraph test, isn't strong enough to generate a false confession.

The time between the inducement and the confession measures the impact of the inducement on the confession. The longer the time that separates the two, the less negative impact the inducement will have on the confession.

Practical lessons/Key points:

1. Avoid using the suspect's "loved ones" as leverage unless you are stating a relevant fact about the loved one's involvement. If the loved one is a clear suspect, discussing the loved one is relevant and makes strategic sense. If the loved one is not a clear suspect, do not play mind games with the suspect because this would constitute an illegal inducement.

2. Do not make promises in exchange for a confession. State facts – there's a difference. If a confession clears a loved one as a suspect, then state that fact. But don't bullshit the suspect by making him think that a confession will save a loved one from being targeted. It is simple common sense and a fundamental of human decency. Do not threaten to implicate an **innocent** loved one as a way to force a confession. Threatening to implicate family is a cardinal sin against human decency. Never fuck around with family. If the family is innocent, leave them alone. Threatening innocent family members is as shameful as it gets.

Strategy/issue #5

Building trust – the line between genuine trust and abuse of trust: Building trust has and always will be a fundamental essential in the truth-seeking process. The issue was a point of contention in the *Oickle* case because the trust the police built contributed to the confession. The issue was whether the police crossed the line. Did they stay inbounds with genuine trust or go out-of-bounds by abusing trust?

The S.C.C. ruled that the police did nothing wrong. The police built the trust in a reassuring manner. The S.C.C. found no act by the police that abused the trust. The Court made a bold statement about the issue of building trust with a suspect in the truth-seeking process:

"Excluding a confession because the police cause the accused to trust them would send a "perverse message" that they should engage only in "adversarial, aggressive questioning to ensure they never gain the suspect's trust."

Translation: Building trust is not evil. Considering gaining a suspect's trust to be manipulative would be counter-intuitive. If building trust was wrong, then being untrustworthy would be right. The defence can't have it both ways. If trust built by the police could be considered an illegal inducement, that would leave the police no alternatives. Building trust is one of the secrets for any relationship to work, including any truth-seeking process whether it's in an interrogation room, a boardroom, a classroom, or living room. The S.C.C. was simply stating the obvious – genuine trust is the desired outcome in any relationship. Trust is an intangible. Trust can't be built without the consent of the suspect. That means that the suspect decides when trust is built. Trust can't be built without his permission. When trust is built, good things happen.

Practical lessons/Key points:

1. Trust doesn't have a generic appearance. Trust is an intangible. Trust is a tacit connection that often can't be fully described by words – a force that motivates the exchange of meaningful dialogue that leads to the truth. Although trust may not look the same in every case, there are immutable truths about trust.

2. Trust can't be built with **A**-bombs – **a**rrogance, **a**nnoyance, **a**ggression, **a**mateurism, **a**ntagonism, and **a**rtificiality. Those are the six main characteristics of The **A**sshole. In other words, assholes can't build trust. I learned this the hard way. Any time I acted like an asshole toward people, they didn't tell the truth. They hid the truth. There's many ways to be an asshole, but the 3-Cs are the worst – **c**ondescending, **c**ondemning, **c**onfrontational. Intolerable cockiness. The 3-Cs are easy to pick out –pretentiousness, being judgmental, conflict-oriented. They top the characteristics list of The Asshole personality. The Asshole doesn't attract the truth. S/he buries it. That said, disingenuous cordiality isn't the answer either. Society tries to condition us to accept blanket softness – warm and fuzzy communication intended to build the biggest friends list on the block and score the most "likes." Being a perpetual bleeding heart isn't the solution to building trust.

    Think of the mentors who have made the biggest positive impact in your life. Some had a great bed-side manner, others didn't. But they all had one thing in common – honesty, the hallmark of the *true professional self.* The second quality is competence. The third is the absence of self-interest. The best mentors you've had are not your friends or cheerleaders. They didn't press "like" to everything you said or did. Mentors built trust primarily because they believed in you and lead you to believe in them. I guarantee that none of your mentors were assholes. The same applies to building trust in the interrogation room – building trust brings out the best. It's never easy but it gets easier. The centerpiece of every successful interrogation always has been and always will be a level of trust, an intangible connection that makes the truth work its way out. I could write a whole book on how to build trust but reading that book or this book will not guarantee that you will master the art of building trust. There's a fine but clear line that separates trust from manipulation. Trust is long-term. It never fails. Manipulation is the abuse of trust. It may work in the short-term but it always leads to hell. Manipulation is the leading strategy of opportunistic sociopaths who don't give a shit about anyone except themselves. All the knowledge in the world won't help opportunistic sociopaths. *True professional self* is the secret behind building trust. Think of doctors, teachers, coaches, bankers, or any other alleged professional who you have trusted or mistrusted. You stuck with those who brought out their true professional self and dropped the bungling amateurs and bullshitters. The same applies to the profession of law enforcement.

Strategy/issue #6

The absence of an "atmosphere of oppression": In this case, the S.C.C. ruled that the police never deprived the accused of food, water, or sleep. No evidence was fabricated. Although the re-enactment was done when the accused had had little sleep, he was already awake and was clearly told that he could stop at any time. The court found "at best mild inducements" that did not create an oppressive environment.

Translation: Don't beat down the suspect mentally. We all know that physically beating down a suspect is obviously illegal and a crime. Mentally beating down a suspect is an illegal inducement because it may cause a false confession as an escape. In ordinary language, an atmosphere of oppression is extreme deprivation that causes a psychological hell through pain, suffering, and loss of dignity. Oppression is inhumane treatment. It's forcing the suspect to be treated like an animal. No confession will be admissible when the suspect's free will has been broken. Oppression is professional bullying. It's sadistic. The S.C.C. never said you need to build a country club atmosphere. You don't have to provide the comforts of a spa. But you can't go overboard and be uncivilized.

Practical lessons/Key points:

1. The S.C.C. did not give concrete guidelines about when suspects have to be fed, how much they have to be fed, and when they need sleep. The key is unreasonable deprivation.

2. Strike the balance between unreasonable hospitality and unreasonable inhospitalty. As with many aspects of criminal law, the word "reasonable" is left abstract to give you discretion about how to treat the suspect humanely within the context of the specific case. A number of factors have to be considered, including, but not limited to the time of day or night, the suspect's condition at the time of the arrest, public safety urgencies, investigative urgencies, and most important, the suspect's state-of-mind in relation to the cognitive ability to exercise free will.

Strategy/issue #7

Failure to inform the suspect about the inadmissibility of polygraph test results: The police failed to clearly inform the accused that polygraph test results are inadmissible in court. The S.C.C. ruled that this failure was insufficient to automatically exclude a confession. The S.C.C. stated the following general rule:

"Failure to inform a suspect about the inadmissibility of a polygraph test will not automatically produce an involuntary confession. By itself, this circumstance will not exclude a confession. Instead, the most it can do is be a factor in the overall voluntariness analysis."

Translation: The S.C.C. gave the police considerable leeway with this ruling. The police should inform the suspect that polygraph test results are inadmissible but it's not a mandatory obligation. The failure to inform the suspect that polygraph test results are inadmissible is only one factor that, in conjunction with other illegal inducements, may exclude a confession. This alone cannot be used to exclude a confession, and it cannot automatically exclude a confession.

Practical lessons/Key points:

1. Prepare a polygraph test "lesson plan" so that you can teach, in simple language, a suspect about the test. Give the suspect literature to accompany your teaching instructions.

2. Explain the rules of evidence and emphasize that the polygraph test results are inadmissible. Ask if he understands that the polygraph test result cannot be used as evidence by the prosecution. Record the answer verbatim.

Strategy/issue #8

Exaggerating the polygraph's validity: The police repeatedly told the accused that the polygraph was an *"infallible determiner of the truth."* The S.C.C. agreed that these are exaggerated claims, considering the existing literature that shows that they are *"far from infallible."* The court referred to a Quebec Court of Appeal decision in *R. v. Amyot* (1990), which concluded that the representation of the polygraph as infallible renders a confession inadmissible. The S.C.C. found that this case was different. In the *Amyot* case, the confession followed the polygraph test results "almost immediately." In this case, *Oickle*, the accused was "not overwhelmed" by the polygraph results.

The issue is whether the polygraph test creates an oppressive atmosphere. Many lower courts have taken varied approaches to determine this. The prominent factor seemingly is whether the test causes *"emotional disintegration."* In this case the accused cried, but this did not constitute emotional disintegration. As a rule, the S.C.C. stated the following:

> *The mere fact that a suspect cries upon confessing is not evidence of "complete emotional disintegration." Tears are to be expected when someone finally divulges they committed a crime – particularly when the suspect is a generally law-abiding and upstanding citizen. Simply confronting the suspect with adverse evidence, like a polygraph test, is not grounds for exclusion.*

Police exaggeration of the reliability or importance of any evidence does not, by itself, render a confession involuntary. *"Eyewitness accounts are by no means infallible."* The S.C.C. has previously ruled admissible a confession made after the police told a suspect they did not believe his denials because several eyewitnesses reported that they saw him commit the offence.

Translation: The S.C.C. gave the police even more leeway with this ruling. I honestly believe the police were referring to the physiological changes that the polygraph test measures, not the polygraph examiner's ability to interpret them, when they referred to infallibility. But that's just my opinion. The accuracy of the physiological changes is not the controversy surrounding polygraph test accuracy. It's the human factor – the polygraph operator's interpretation skills. The S.C.C. gave considerable leeway – the police don't have to be 100% accurate when they inform the suspect about the strength of evidence. The S.C.C. was very generous with the police about how they communicated the importance of specific evidence.

Practical lessons/Key points:

1. Despite the considerable leeway, don't take advantage of it. Be 100% positive about what you tell a suspect regarding the strength of evidence. Your credibility is at stake. You might get away with exaggerations about the strength of evidence but eventually your credibility will suffer.

2. In reality, exaggerations are completely unnecessary. The strength of evidence doesn't need stretching. It's easy to doubt the true strength of the evidence of a specific case because of past conditioning; there's a tendency to underestimate the true value. Change the focus, change the outcome. Instead of exaggerating the strength of evidence, let the suspect make his own conclusion. Chances are he may exaggerate the strength of the evidence on his own and you will keep your credibility intact.

Misleading the accused regarding the duration of the interrogation: At issue in this case was misleading the accused about the expected duration of the polygraph test and about the length of interrogation that follows a failed test. Additionally, the Criminal Lawyers' Association argued that the police should clearly separate post-test interrogation from the test itself instead of conducting immediate intense questioning. The S.C.C. rejected these arguments, ruling that none of these circumstances render a confession involuntary.

Translation: More leeway to the police. The police don't have to be 100% accurate about clock management. They don't have to give the suspect a precise schedule of events. And the police don't have to take a break between the polygraph test and the post-polygraph test interrogation. Down time at the end of a polygraph test is not mandatory or even recommended by the S.C.C.

Practical lessons/Key points:

1. Create a reasonable schedule when the suspect consents to a polygraph test.

2. Inform the accused of reasonable time expectations but you don't have to be 100% correct. You don't have time constraints. If you're wrong about the time frame, overtime won't automatically exclude a confession.

Conclusion – Interrogation Issues

This chapter focused on the circumstances of the *Oickle* case and the rulings specifically related to the nine interrogation issues. However the *Oickle* decision goes deeper. There is more to the judgment that will be discussed in the next chapter. -

These are conclusions reached about the rulings concerning the nine interrogation issues:

1. In many ways, the interrogation in the *Oickle* case was typical. Most of the strategies were common practices that had been used forever. Nothing was new or innovative. The interrogation issues were common. Essentially, the S.C.C. validated and confirmed nine common interrogation practices and routine issues. That, by itself, represents valuable investigation benefits and advantages.

2. The *Oickle* interrogation represents a basic interrogation playbook but not a complete one. It doesn't include every conceivable interrogation issue or practice. *Oickle* doesn't limit the police to these practices. Far from it. The S.C.C. ruled only on what the police used in this case. The remainder of the judgment, explained in the next chapter, provides guidelines for the rest of the interrogation playbook.

3. The *Oickle* interrogation is a point-of-reference that you can use to plan your interrogations. The decision gives flexible boundaries. The S.C.C. is not expecting perfection but they do expect reasonable limits of inappropriate inducements. There's a line that you can't cross but the S.C.C. didn't paint the perfect line of demarcation. The line depends on the context of each case. But the *Oickle* decision gives one point-of-reference example of how you can stay inbounds.

4. The police have nothing to complain about. They were given considerable leeway by the S.C.C. Next time you're tempted to complain that the laws are against the police, review *Oickle*.

5. Even though *Oickle* gives you a point-of-reference playbook, don't expect guaranteed results even if you copy the interrogation plan word-for-word. Here's the reason: Two people can say the exact same things but never get the exact same results. Words are not created equal. The content may be the same but *how* words are said is the difference. ***Communication style*** is the primary key to the outcome of any interrogation. Content is in second place. You can say all the right words but the wrong communication style leads to wrong impact, leading to the wrong outcome. Two people can say the exact same words to the exact same group but you won't get the same outcome because everyone has a personalized communication style and communication style is the leading cause of positive impact or negative impact on the audience. Subsequent chapters will explain why this happens and the research to back it up.

6. *Oickle* is a landmark decision more for what didn't happen than what did. What is easily forgotten is that a lower court, a provincial Court of Appeal, had thrown out the confession. Never forget that the Nova Scotia Court of Appeal excluded the confession. They saw the interrogation differently than the S.C.C. This is a perfect example of inconsistency. It's a perfect example of how top legal experts can analyze the exact same case and reach polar opposite decisions. Even though the S.C.C. has more authority and reversed the bad call, don't forget how difficult it is for legal experts in the CJS to reach a consensus on interrogations you conduct. Objectivity is not created equal. That will never change.

I can't overstate the significance of the S.C.C. overruling the Nova Scotia Court of Appeal rulings. If the case had never gone to the S.C.C. or if the S.C.C. had not overturned the decision, interrogation as we know it would never have been the same. If the S.C.C. had confirmed the lower court's decision, the interrogation landscape would have undergone a seismic shift; interrogation limits would have boxed you in, confining you inside the smallest of playing fields. That's why *Oickle* is epic – what didn't happen had a bigger impact than what did.

Chapter 8
Oickle Part 2: The Contemporary Confessions Rule – Preventing forced and false confessions

The previous chapter explained what the S.C.C. ruled in relation to the specific interrogation. This is a short chapter that summarizes the "Contemporary Confessions Rule" in two parts:

i. an annotated translation of the Contemporary Confessions Rule straight from *Oickle* with 6 key points that translate the rule, and;

ii. two charts that illustrate

      a. the interaction of voluntary and reliable, and;

      b. four factors that determine voluntary and reliable.

The following is the direct quote straight from the *Oickle* judgment that creates the Contemporary Confessions Rule:

> *"The common law confessions rule is well-suited to protect against false confessions. While its overriding concern is with voluntariness, this concept overlaps with reliability. A confession that is not voluntary will often (though not always) be unreliable. The application of the rule will by necessity be contextual. Hard and fast rules simply cannot account for the variety of circumstances that vitiate the voluntariness of a confession, and would inevitably result in a rule that would be both over- and under-inclusive. A trial judge should therefore consider all the relevant factors when reviewing a confession."*

Translation:

1. The Contemporary Confessions Rule added the concept of "reliability" to the concept of "voluntary." *Voluntary* refers to *how* a confession was elicited. It asks the question, *"Did the suspect freely say it?"* "Reliability" refers to the credibility of the final product (confession). It asks the questions, *"Is this confession <u>the truth</u>? Can it be believed? Is it a false confession or not?"*

    The goal of the Contemporary Confessions Rule is stated two ways: (i) the <u>prevention of forced and false confessions</u> (ii) the discovery of the truth. The addition of reliability to the Confessions Rule is a common-sense safe-guard to protect the innocent from being charged and convicted but it's not a shield to protect criminals from hiding the truth. The goal of the Contemporary Confessions Rule is to paint boundaries to make sure that "threats-to-society" don't walk away scot-free. The boundaries are intended to ensure civility and prevent barbarism, on both sides of the interrogation room.

2. "Voluntariness" remains at the core but it now joins, interacts, and overlaps with "reliability" despite being a separate concept. The key point is that an involuntary confession will often be unreliable, but not always. This means a forced confession <u>may</u> be a false confession (unreliable) or, it may be a true confession (reliable). In order to be admissible, the Crown has the onus to prove, beyond a reasonable doubt, that the confession was both voluntary and reliable. Failure to prove either one results in mandatory exclusion.

3. *Contextual analysis* of every interrogation is the key. This means admissibility is decided case-by-case because of the <u>uniqueness</u> of every interrogation. The specific context of every interrogation will determine the admissibility, not "hard-and-fast rules." This is the perfect solution to the problem of interrogation uniqueness. Every interrogation has its own brand, its own unique character. A cookie-cutter approach to admissibility analysis isn't the solution. What is said in one interrogation may be proper but improper in another interrogation. What is said and what is done during an investigation has to be considered within the context of that interrogation's uniqueness.

4. The flexibility of contextual analysis is intended to *fit the situation.* Contextual analysis is a wide-lens approach to evaluating an interrogation. It takes in the big picture instead of a narrow view that focuses only on isolated moments during an interrogation. This results in "balancing the playing field and the rule book. " Neither side gets an advantage. Equality of rules is the intention, not a one-sided rulebook.

5. Every relevant factor in an interrogation must be weighed. That means that no relevant factor can be discounted; each one counts. The accountability of every relevant factor leads to a system of checks and balances as oversight to eliminate injustices, on both sides. Conversely, a trial judge cannot focus on just one relevant factor and ignore the rest. Big picture, not just a fraction of it.

6. The Contemporary Confessions Rule is a triple-purpose Protection Plan:

   a. it protects innocent people from confessing falsely to crimes they didn't commit;

   b. it protects the police from causing a false confession, and

   c. it protects the police from being falsely accused of causing a false confession when a confession is the truth.

The Contemporary Confessions Rule is both an acknowledgement and solution to the problem of false confessions. It is not a one-side perspective. It is not an indictment on the police. It is evolution. The new Contemporary Confessions Rule formalizes all the elements that contribute to forced and false confessions – improper inducements, oppression, operating mind, trickery. None of these elements were new. All of them had been introduced during the century of case law that caused the evolution of the Traditional Confessions Rule. *Oickle* put it all in one rulebook by expanding the Traditional Confessions Rule from only threats and promises to include oppression, operating mind, and police trickery. The following diagrams demonstrate the evolution from a one-element definition of "voluntariness" in the Tradition Confessions Rule to the broader version with 4 elements in the Contemporary Confessions Rule that emerged from *Oickle*.

Traditional Confessions Rule

Voluntary = absence of threats and promises

Contemporary Confessions Rule

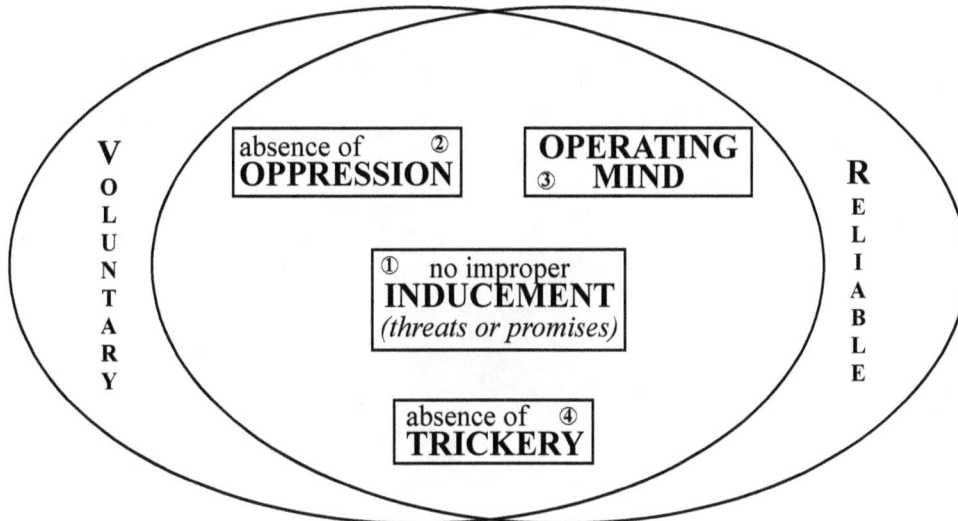

V O L U N T A R Y

absence of ② **OPPRESSION**

③ **OPERATING MIND**

① no improper **INDUCEMENT** *(threats or promises)*

absence of ④ **TRICKERY**

R E L I A B L E

The diagram above shows the connection and interplay of the 4 "Force Factors;" those that determine if a confession made to a PIA is reliable and voluntary, or not.

1. **Absence** of illegal inducements – threats or promises

2. **Absence** of oppression

3. **Absence** of police trickery

4. Presence of an operating mind

An admissible confession to a person in authority (PIN), has to encompass Force Factor #4 while being free from the first 3 Force Factors – forces that compel a person to confess against his will or force him to confess falsely in order to escape the hell of intolerable conditions. These first 3 Force Factors are physical and psychological attacks that break down "free will." They are illegal, unnatural forces that generate a confession outside of the suspect's own self-generated natural force – the conscience.

As will be explained in subsequent Chapterrs, the 4 factors work within the **context** of each specific interrogation. Even though they are the primary elements that define and govern both concepts of voluntary and reliability, the Confessions Rule must be applied *contextually*. This means that there are no precise, concrete rules that apply in every case. The 4 factors serve as a *general* guideline only. The S.C.C. emphasized that hard-and-fast rules cannot be rigidly set because strict, inflexible rules could not possibly account for the endless possible circumstances associated with every interrogation and confession.

Chapter 9
Force Factor #1: Threats or Promises – Improper Inducements

This chapter is longer than the rest because the concept of threats and promises as improper inducements is a lengthy part of the *Oickle* judgment which I have broken down into 9 Rulings. This chapter is written in annotated form – the verbatim quote from the judgment followed by a translation of key points. The next Chapter stays on the topic of threats and promises with a <u>practical application</u> explanation:

Ruling #1: *"Threats or Promises. This is of course the core of the confessions rule from Ibrahim, supra. It is therefore important to define precisely what types of threats or promises will raise a reasonable doubt as to the voluntariness of a confession. While obviously imminent threats of torture will render a confession inadmissible, most cases will not be so clear."*

Translation:

i. "Threats or promises" remain the central core of the Confessions Rule.

ii. A "threat or promise" constitutes and improper inducement.

iii. An improper inducement generally excludes a confession to a PIA.

iv. Creating a definitive list of what specifically constitutes a "threat or promise" isn't easy, is impractical, and likely will never happen. However, at the top of the list of concrete circumstances that qualify as a "threat or promise" is the obvious – violence – physical abuse or the threat of it. Torture, the threat of torture, any actual physical force, or threat of physical force all are 100% improper inducements.

v. Physical abuse or the threat of it <u>will</u> exclude a confession. Mandatory exclusion for violence – no discretion, no exemptions, no leeway, no what-ifs.

vi. The rest of the list won't be clear. The only clear, undisputed threat or promise that qualifies on the what-never-to-do list of improper inducements is physical abuse or the threat or it. Other than torture and the threat of torture, inducements are contextual, meaning they may be classified as improper or proper depending on how they fit in the interrogation – the effect they have on free will, whether or not they constitute a strong enough quid pro quo to force a confession or force a false confession.

Ruling #2: *"As noted above, in Ibrahim the Privy Council ruled that statements would be inadmissible if they were the result of "fear of prejudice or hope of advantage". The classic "hope of advantage" is the prospect of leniency from the courts. It is improper for a person in authority to suggest to a suspect that he or she will take steps to procure a reduced charge or sentence if the suspect confesses. Therefore in Nugent, supra, the court excluded the statement of a suspect who was told that if he confessed, the charge could be reduced from murder to manslaughter. See also R. v. Kalashnikoff (1981), 57 C.C.C. (2d) 481 (B.C.C.A.); R. v. Lazure (1959), 126 C.C.C. 331 (Ont. C.A.); R. J. Marin, Admissibility of Statements (9th ed. (loose-leaf)), at p. 1–15. Intuitively implausible as it may seem, both judicial precedent and academic authority confirm that the pressure of intense and prolonged questioning may convince a suspect that no one will believe his or her protestations of innocence, and that a conviction is inevitable. In these circumstances, holding out the possibility of a reduced charge or sentence in exchange for a confession would raise a reasonable doubt as to the voluntariness of any ensuing confession. An explicit offer by the police to procure lenient treatment in return for a confession is clearly a very strong inducement, and will warrant exclusion in all but exceptional circumstances."*

Translation:

This verbatim ruling is confusing. It discusses two circumstances that qualify as improper inducements/threats or promises: offer of leniency and prolonged interrogation. But only the offer of leniency has a specific exemption to mandatory exclusion. Adding to the confusion is the way the S.C.C. discussed the consequences of prolonged interrogation – alone and in conjunction with offers of leniency. Depending on how you read it, offers of leniency are improper inducements either alone or during prolonged interrogation.

i. A PIA's offer of leniency in exchange for a confession has a special designation – it's an improper inducement with strong likelihood of exclusion, not mandatory exclusion.

ii. Don't confuse the non-mandatory exclusion as considerable leeway. It's a weak, uncommon exemption that will rarely be used. But, the possibility of admission does exist even though the possibility is remote. The key to the exemption that allows admission is the phrase "exceptional circumstances." Not only was no concrete definition given, there was no hint of what could qualify as "exceptional circumstances" that would admit a confession induced by an offer of leniency.

iii. PIAs don't have plea bargaining authority during an interrogation. A plea bargain in exchange for a confession is improper and will very likely exclude the confession.

iv. Strength matters. How strong an inducement is determines whether it will be improper or not and whether it will exclude or not. Leniency as a deal for a confession is classified as a "very strong inducement."

Ruling #3: *(This is not a typo, it's repeated for a reason) "Intuitively implausible as it may seem, both judicial precedent and academic authority confirm that the pressure of intense and prolonged questioning may convince a suspect that no one will believe his or her protestations of innocence, and that a conviction is inevitable. In these circumstances, holding out the possibility of a reduced charge or sentence in exchange for a confession would raise a reasonable doubt as to the voluntariness of any ensuing confession. An explicit offer by the police to procure lenient treatment in return for a confession is clearly a very strong inducement, and will warrant exclusion in all but exceptional circumstances."*

Translation:

i. The first sentence, by itself, clearly states that the stress of "intense and prolonged interrogation" may cause a false confession. But the skepticism of the opening phrase – *"Intuitively implausible as it may seem"* – contradicts it. It seems that the S.C.C. is acknowledging the negative influences of intense and prolonged interrogation, with reservation.

ii. Reading the first sentence in conjunction with the second sentence raises the severity of intense and prolonged interrogation when it includes offers of leniency or fear of prejudice.

iii. Either way, an intense and prolonged interrogation will likely be an improper inducement. The problem is the lack of a concrete definition or any hint of a time frame that is acceptable or not. The reason why the S.C.C. won't impose a time-clock to interrogation goes back to its stance on "hard and fast rules." The duration of every interrogation will be contextually analyzed to determine whether or not it is an improper inducement. Duration is one contextual factor. The same applies to the concept of "intensity." Case law research is needed to discover examples of what does and does not qualify as "intense."

iv. The S.C.C. only referred to an offer of leniency in this passage. Fear of prejudice was addressed in the next quote.

Ruling #4: *"The Ibrahim rule speaks not only of "hope of advantage", but also of "fear of prejudice". Obviously, any confession that is the product of outright violence is involuntary and unreliable, and therefore inadmissible. More common, and more challenging judicially, are the more subtle, veiled threats that can be used against suspects. The Honourable Fred Kaufman, in the third edition of The Admissibility of Confessions (1979), at p. 230, provides a useful starting point:*

> *Threats come in all shapes and sizes. Among the most common are words to the effect that "it would be better" to tell, implying thereby that dire consequences might flow from a refusal to talk. Maule J. recognized this fact, and said that "there can be no doubt that such words, if spoken by a competent person, have been held to exclude a confession at least 500 times" (R. v. Garner (1848), 3 Cox C.C. 175, at p. 177).*

Courts have accordingly excluded confessions made in response to police suggestions that it would be better if they confessed. See R. v. Desmeules, [1971] R.L. 505 (Que. Ct. Sess. P.); Comeau v. The Queen (1961), 131 C.C.C. 139 (N.S.S.C.); Lazure, supra; R. v. Hanlon (1958), 28 C.R. 398 (Nfld. C.A.), at p. 401; White, supra, at p. 129.

However, phrases like "it would be better if you told the truth" should not automatically require exclusion. Instead, as in all cases, the trial judge must examine the entire context of the confession, and ask whether there is a reasonable doubt that the resulting confession was involuntary. Freedman C.J.M. applied this approach correctly in R. v. Puffer (1976), 31 C.C.C. (2d) 81 (Man. C.A.). In that case a suspect in a robbery and murder asked to meet with two police officers of his acquaintance. At this meeting, one officer said: "The best thing you can do is come in with us and tell the truth" (p. 95). Freedman C.J.M. held that while the officer's language was "unfortunate", it did not require exclusion (at p. 95): "McFall wanted to talk, he wanted to give the police his version of what had occurred, and above all he did not want Puffer and Kizyma to get away, leaving him to face the music alone" (emphasis in original).

In his reasons, Freedman C.J.M. referred to a passage from an article he had written earlier, "Admissions and Confessions", published in Salhany and Carter, eds., Studies in Canadian Criminal Evidence (1972), at pp. 110-11, where he stated the following:

> *Risky though it be for a policeman to use words like "better tell us everything"— and an experienced and conscientious officer will shun them like the plague — their consequences will not always be fatal. There have been some instances where words of that type have been employed, and yet a confession following thereon has been admitted. That may occur when the court is satisfied that the offending words, potentially perilous though they be, did not in fact induce the accused to speak. In other words, he would have confessed in any event, the court's enquiry on the point establishing that his statement was indeed voluntarily made. It is scarcely necessary to emphasize, however, that cases of the kind just mentioned will confront a prosecuting counsel with special difficulty. For words like "better tell the truth" carry the mark of an inducement on their very face, and a resultant confession may well find itself battling against the stream.*

This Court upheld the Court of Appeal's ruling. See McFall v. The Queen, [1980] 1 S.C.R. 321; see also R. v. Hayes (1982), 65 C.C.C. (2d) 294 (Alta. C.A.), at pp. 296-97. I agree that "it would be better" comments require exclusion only where the circumstances reveal an implicit threat or promise.

Translation:

i. The opposite of a promise of leniency is the fear of prejudice, the fear of consequences for failure to confess. "If you don't confess, you'll get the maximum penalty." If you don't confess, you'll never get out of jail." "If you don't confess, you'll get a beating." Or the threat can be disguised with veiled threats including but not limited to, "You'd better confess."

ii. Clear threats and veiled threats are the same – they are improper inducements.

iii. Outright violence automatically excludes a confession. There are no exceptions to exclusion of a confession that follows violence of any kind. Same rule applies to clear threats or veiled threats.

iv. The word "better" *may* be a veiled threat and *may* qualify as an improper inducement if the trial judge considers the word "better" within the entire context, to be an implied threat of consequences – violent or legal. "Better" is not the only example of a veiled threat. There are countless examples. They come in "all shapes and sizes." There is no definitive list of what to say and what not to say. Case law research will give examples to make those lists.

v. The word "better" does not qualify as an automatic improper inducement and it does not carry mandatory exclusion. "Better" allows discretionary classification as improper or proper inducement and exclusion/admission is also discretionary. The decision is based on the effect of "better" within the entire context. The trial judge is required to analyze the entire context, not just the isolated use of "better," and determine if the word induced the confession. The key is whether the suspect would have confessed regardless if "better" was used.

vi. Using the word "better" during an interrogation is a risk. Even though it doesn't carry mandatory exclusion, the passage from the court document (above) is a caution to not use it. To be on the safe side, remove "better" from your interrogation vocabulary.

vii. Hanging a harsher sentence over the suspect's head if he doesn't confess is an improper inducement that will exclude a confession. So will the threat of any consequence that makes the proceedings worse – more charges, severity of charges, pre-trial custody. A confession made out of fear of legal consequences is involuntary. Thrown out.

Ruling #5: *"Another type of inducement relevant to this appeal is an offer of psychiatric assistance or other counselling for the suspect in exchange for a confession. While this is clearly an inducement, it is not as strong as an offer of leniency and regard must be had to the entirety of the circumstances. A good example of this comes from R. v. Ewert (1991), 68 C.C.C. (3d) 207 (B.C.C.A.). In that case, the police made what Hinkson J.A. at the Court of Appeal described as a "bold offer to the accused to help him, in the sense of providing psychiatric help, if he told them what had happened" (p. 216). Reversing the Court of Appeal, this Court upheld the trial judge's conclusion that, while the police conduct was an inducement, it was not a factor in the suspect's decision to confess. Ewert thus recognizes the importance of a contextual approach."*

Translation:

i. An offer of professional help is not the same as an offer of leniency. They have different strength levels. Offers for professional help are inducements but weaker than offers of leniency.

ii. An offer of professional help is not automatically an improper inducement. It does not carry mandatory exclusion.

iii. The key factor is whether the offer for professional help was a motivating factor in the suspect's decision to confess. Did the offer make up the suspect's mind to confess?

iv. The line between an improper and proper inducement is the presence or absence of quid pro quo. Imposing conditions to an offer of professional help is wrong. Not imposing conditions to an offer of professional help is right. If professional help is conditional on a confession, it will likely be an improper inducement. Offering professional help as bait in exchange for a confession will likely exclude the confession. If the offer for professional help is unconditional, isolated and disconnected from a confession, the confession will likely be safe.

Ruling #6: *"Threats or promises need not be aimed directly at the suspect for them to have a coercive effect. For example, in R. v. Jackson (1977), 34 C.C.C. (2d) 35 (B.C.C.A.), McIntyre J.A. (as he then was) addressed a confession obtained in a case where the accused and his friend Winn had robbed and murdered a hitchhiker. The police suspected the murder was Jackson's doing, and urged him to confess, lest his friend Winn be unjustly convicted of murder. The trial judge had concluded that:*

> *[The police] were exerting a subtle form of pressure on Jackson, they were appealing to his concept of right and wrong... They indicated that unless they got to the truth of the matter, it might be necessary to charge both, and this too was a very likely possibility. The officers were completely frank with him. The officers hoped that when Jackson was faced with what they had, and what might transpire if he didn't speak up, that he would take Winn off the hook and confess. That is exactly what he did. I can see nothing in what they said or in what they did that can be construed by Jackson as holding out the possibility of any benefit to him should he confess.*

McIntyre J.A. agreed that no hope of advantage that would render a confession inadmissible had been held out to the accused. He then presented the following very helpful analysis of the law (at p. 38):

> *[Cases] must be considered in relation to their own facts. It is my opinion that for a promised benefit to a person other than the accused to vitiate a confession, the benefit must be of such a nature that when considered in the light of the relationship between the person and the accused, and all the surrounding circumstances of the confession, it would tend to induce the accused to make an untrue statement, for it is the danger that a person may be induced by promises to make such a statement which lies at the root of this exclusionary rule.*

McIntyre J.A. offered, as examples of improper inducements, telling a mother that her daughter would not be charged with shoplifting if the mother confessed to a similar offence (see Commissioners of Customs and Excise v. Harz, [1967] 1 A.C. 760 (H.L.), at p. 821), or a sergeant-major keeping a company on parade until he learned who was responsible for a stabbing (see R. v. Smith, [1959] 2 Q.B. 35). In Jackson, by contrast, the accused had merely known Winn for a year in prison. The offence occurred a few days after their release. Neither testified to a relationship such that "the immunity of one was of such vital concern to the other that he would untruthfully confess to preserve it" (p. 39). The confession was therefore admissible."

Translation:

i.   A third part inducement is a threat or promise aimed at another person other than the suspect. It's directing a consequence or benefit to a person other than a suspect. Example: "We will/won't charge your sister if you do/don't confess."

ii. Third party inducements may a problem or they may be a solution.

iii. Third part inducements may be improper or proper, depending on whether they induce true or false confessions.

iv. The decision to classify a third part inducement as improper or proper depends on how it's used within the context of the entire interrogation. If it's used to appeal to the suspect's sense of right from wrong to get the truth, the third part inducement will likely be proper. If it's used to offer leniency or cause fear of prejudice, the third party inducement will be improper and will cause exclusion of the confession.

v.   Third party threats or promises are inducements but they are not automatically improper. They may be classified as proper inducements. They don't carry mandatory exclusion. Admission/exclusion is discretionary. The classification of the third party inducement as proper or improper depends on the coercive strength of the inducement.

vi. The coercive strength of a third party inducement is connected to the type of relationship and the suspect's desire and commitment to protect and preserve that relationship. The level of the suspect's emotional attachment to the third party determines how far the suspect will go to protect the relationship, particularly by falsely confessing to a crime that the suspect was innocent of.

Ruling #7: *"The final threat or promise relevant to this appeal is the use of **moral or spiritual inducements**. These inducements will generally not produce an involuntary confession, for the very simple reason that the inducement offered is not in the control of the police officers. If a police officer says "If you don't confess, you'll spend the rest of your life in jail. Tell me what happened and I can get you a lighter sentence", then clearly there is a strong, and improper, inducement for the suspect to confess. The officer is offering a quid pro quo, and it raises the possibility that the suspect is confessing not because of any **internal desire to confess,** but merely in order to gain the benefit offered by the interrogator. By contrast, with most spiritual inducements the interrogator has no control over the suggested benefit. If a police officer convinces a suspect that he will feel better if he confesses, the officer has not offered anything. I therefore agree with Kaufman, supra, who summarized the jurisprudence as follows at p. 186:*

> *We may therefore conclude that, as a <u>general rule</u>, confessions which result from spiritual exhortations or **appeals to conscience** and morality, are <u>admissible</u> in evidence, <u>whether urged by a person in authority or by someone else</u>. [Emphasis in original.]"*

Translation:

The most important lessons to learn about interrogation are in the above verbatim quote from Oickle, that I've titled "Ruling #7." I have bolded and underlined rules and phrases that you will need to understand throughout all interrogation training.

i. <u>Moral or spiritual inducements are proper inducements.</u>

ii. Generally, confessions resulting from moral and spiritual inducements are voluntary. The S.C.C. left the door slightly open for possible exclusion by making it a general rule, not a mandatory rule. Trial judges do have discretion to rule morally-induced confessions involuntary but it will be rarely used based on the language of the above ruling. The only way a moral inducement will be classified as improper is if the police somehow make it conditional by attaching a quid pro quo, by making the suspect believe that the police somehow control the benefit which, in itself, seems counter-intuitive.

iii. The best example of a moral or spiritual inducement is an **appeal to conscience**.

iv. **Appealing to the conscience is the cornerstone of interrogation strategy.** Learn how to appeal to the conscience and you will be a superstar interrogator. Appealing to the conscience is the most important interrogation strategy because it's legal and ethical. The reason is control – the police have no control over "most" moral and spiritual benefits.

v. The S.C.C. acknowledged the psychological theory of the <u>compulsion to confess</u> with the phrase **"internal desire to confess."** Here are the key points to this acknowledgment:

- The inner compulsion to confess is real, not just a psychological theory.

- The inner compulsion to confess is a natural force that induces a confession through the natural internal <u>desire</u> to admit a wrongdoing.

- The inner compulsion to confess does not constitute a quid pro quo because it is the opposite of one.

- The inner compulsion to confess is the legally preferred inducement.

- Confessions resulting from the internal desire to confess are <u>self-generated.</u>

- Self-generated confessions are generally voluntary and generally admissible.

- Be careful of using the phrase "feel better" by itself because it may be construed as the possibility of avoiding physical pain. Add the word "internally" or "spiritually" or "inside" to clarify what exactly will feel better if the suspect confesses.

vi. The S.C.C. gave two more examples of what never to say – improper inducements that will exclude a confession to a PIA:

- *"If you don't confess, you'll spend the rest of your life in jail;* and,

- *Tell me what happened and I can get you a lighter sentence."*

Emphasis on the last paragraph of the Ruling #7:

<u>General rule:</u> *"Confessions which result from spiritual exhortations or **appeals to conscience** and morality, are <u>admissible</u> in evidence, <u>whether urged by a person in authority or by someone else</u>."*

Keep this with you at all times. Read it often. Commit it to memory. Constantly reminding yourself of this general rule is the biggest difference between interrogation failure and success.

> Editorial: The most compelling message to all interrogation critics is the phrase "internal desire to confess." The S.C.C. used the word "desire." A desire is a personal need. We humans don't resist needs, we fight to achieve them especially when an ordinary need becomes a basic survival need. If you have to debate an interrogation critic, your strongest argument is the S.C.C.'s use of "internal desire to confess." The desire to confess is a <u>natural</u> need. Therefore, confessions are not unnatural occurrences.

Ruling #8: *"In summary, courts must remember that the police may often offer some kind of inducement to the suspect to obtain a confession. Few suspects will spontaneously confess to a crime. In the vast majority of cases, the police will have to somehow convince the suspect that it is in his or her best interests to confess. This becomes improper only when the inducements, whether standing alone or in combination with other factors, are strong enough to raise a reasonable doubt about whether the will of the subject has been overborne. On this point I found the following passage from R. v. Rennie (1981), 74 Cr. App. R. 207 (C.A.), at p. 212, particularly apt:*

> *Very few confessions are inspired solely by remorse. Often the motives of an accused are mixed and include a hope that an early admission may lead to an earlier release or a lighter sentence. If it were the law that the mere presence of such a motive, even if promoted by something said or done by a person in authority, led inexorably to the exclusion of a confession, nearly every confession would be rendered inadmissible. This is not the law. In some cases the hope may be self-generated. If so, it is irrelevant, even if it provides the dominant motive for making the confession. In such a case the confession will not have been obtained by anything said or done by a person in authority. More commonly the presence of such a hope will, in part at least, owe its origin to something said or done by such a person. There can be few prisoners who are being firmly but fairly questioned in a police station to whom it does not occur that they might be able to bring both their interrogation and their detention to an earlier end by confession."*

Translation:

i. The S.C.C. acknowledged that confessions usually need: (i) interrogation; and, (ii) inducements. The inducements they are referring to are those considered minor improper inducements such as "best interest" inducements – the type of inducements that are self-generated or low-level PIA-generated "hope of leniency" that is produced by an operating, functional free will. The most common type of hope of leniency is PIA-generated.

ii. The mere presence of hope of leniency is not enough to exclude. Many offenders are motivated to confess by self-generated hope of leniency or low-level PIA-generated hope of leniency. The S.C.C. acknowledged that if there was a zero tolerance policy regarding hope of leniency, including PIA-generated, almost all confessions would be excluded. It would be almost impossible to admit any confession.

iii. Self-generated hope and low-level PIA generated hope are not improper inducements as long as they don't cross the line. The line is the difference between free will overborne and free will not overborne.

iv. Confessions will be excluded when an improper inducement by itself or combined with other factors raise reasonable doubt about whether the suspect's free will was overborne. Overborne is defined in the dictionary as overcome by emotional pressure or physical force.

v. Ruling #8 stretches police leeway and stretches the line that can't be crossed. The condition of overborne free will is drastic mental deterioration. As long as the suspect's free will remains in working order and the hope of leniency stays within reasonable limits, the admissibility of a confession won't be jeopardized.

Ruling #9: *"The most important consideration in all cases is to look for a quid pro quo offer by interrogators, regardless of whether it comes in the form of a threat or a promise."*

Translation:

i. The search for the deal is the number one mission of a trial judge.

ii. The number one factor that decides whether a threat or promise is an improper inducement and whether a confession is excluded is the presence or absence of a quid pro quo offer – an offer to exchange something, good or bad, for a confession.

iii. The S.C.C. does not want interrogations to become a bartering system where confessions are traded for a price.

Chapter 10
Force Factor #1: Threats or Promises – Improper Inducements Part 2: The Inducement Chart

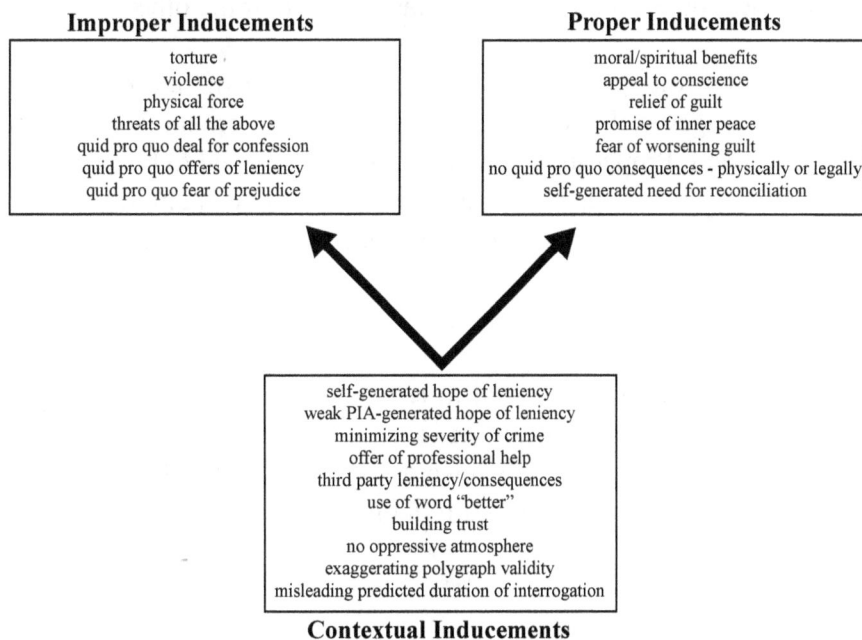

"You can't say that. It's an inducement." The biggest problem with processing *Oickle* rulings is the past use of the word "inducement." The way we used to use the word "inducement" before *Oickle* is the biggest challenge in teaching it, learning it, and putting it into practice in the present. I decided to create Part 2 of Force Factor #1 before explaining the remaining three Force Factors – oppression, trickery, and operating mind – because of the need to change how we use the word "inducement" and because of the volume of rulings that deal with this Factor.

The focus of this chapter is the Inducement Chart. It forms the basis of the Canadian interrogation playbook that illustrates what to do and what not to do. This chapter includes practical lessons and key points that are supplements to the annotated translations, intended to clarify and simply the Threats & Promises rulings:

Lesson 1

The Inducement Chart is the basis of the Interrogation Playbook. It includes what to do and what not to do: two classifications of inducements and three lists. The improper inducements and proper inducement listed are from the original Traditional Confessions Rule. Contextual inducements are inducements in the middle that can go either way. Contextual inducements have to end up as improper or proper. They can't remain permanently in the middle.

Improper inducements are the what-not-to-do list. Proper inducements are the what-to-do list. Both lists keep growing as case law evolves. This list below shows how the list of proper inducements grew from *Oickle*. The contextual inducements listed below all ended up as proper inducements because of *Oickle*. This Chart is not the complete, definitive list of contextual, improper or proper inducements. Far from it. The chart keeps growing throughout the rest of this book series. The chart below is only the beginning – phase one. It's the starting point from *Oickle*.

INDUCEMENT CHART

Improper Inducements	Proper Inducements
torture	moral/spiritual benefits
violence	appeal to conscience
physical force	relief of guilt
threats of all the above	promise of inner peace
quid pro quo deal for confession	fear of worsening guilt
quid pro quo offers of leniency	no quid pro quo consequences - physically or legally
quid pro quo fear of prejudice	self-generated need for reconciliation

Contextual Inducements

self-generated hope of leniency
weak PIA-generated hope of leniency
minimizing severity of crime
offer of professional help
third party leniency/consequences
use of word "better"
building trust
no oppressive atmosphere
exaggerating polygraph validity
misleading predicted duration of interrogation

Lesson 2

As stated in the introduction to this Chapter, the first problem that needs to be clarified is caused by the past use of the word "inducement." In the past, before *Oickle*, we used the word by itself to mean "improper inducement." We didn't use the words "proper" or "improper" in front of inducement. The short form use is the source of confusion.

Lesson 3

Using the word "inducement" by itself to describe improper inducement has its origins in case law over fifty years ago when "voluntary" was originally defined in the Traditional Confessions Rule as "free from inducement."[47] The S.C.C., in *Oickle*, modified the definition to "free from *improper* inducement"[48] which means:

i.   Not all inducements are bad. Before *Oickle*, the word "inducement" implied only wrongdoing – improper or illegal acts. That's not the case now. There are bad inducements and good inducements – improper and proper. The word inducement means anything said or done that is the *cause* of or *reason* for a confession. An inducement is the motivating force(s), good or bad, right or wrong, that influence,persuade, or motivate a suspect to confess. An inducement is any catalyst that triggers or produces a confession.

ii. Every confession is the product of an inducement. What matters is whether the inducement was improper or proper. A right or wrong motivating force induces every confession.

iii. There are two classifications of inducements: improper and proper, but there are three lists of inducements – improper, proper, and contextual. Contextual inducements are inducements that go either way. They may end up classified as improper or proper depending on how the trial judge evaluates the inducement within the context of the entire interrogation. The 2 classification/3 list concept is the same concept as classifying offences – there are 2 classifications (indictable and summary conviction) and a list of offences in the middle (dual procedure) that can go either way as indictable or summary conviction. Contextual inducements are the equivalent of dual procedure offences. Both start out on the middle list without a classification and end up as one classification or the other.

iv. The new definition of "voluntary" marks a shift in the use of interrogation language. The word inducement alone no longer exclusively means improper inducement. We now use proper inducement and improper inducement. Proper inducement replaces what used to be called "no inducement." For example, we used to say that an appeal to the conscience was not an inducement. We meant that it was not an improper inducement. We never called it a "proper inducement" until after *Oickle*.

Lesson 4

The source – inner and outer inducement – is vital to *Oickle* language. Inner inducement is self-generated, conscience-driven. Inner reward is the benefit of an inner inducement. Outer or external inducements are PIA-generated and consequence-driven or externally reward-driven. Inducements remain the core of interrogation, of confessions, of the truth, and of voluntariness and reliability.

---

47   Boudreau v. The King (1949), 94 C.C.C. 1 (S.C.C.).
48   R. v. Oickle (2000), File No. 26535 (S.C.C.).

Confessions don't just happen. Every confession is motivated by a force – inner or outer inducement. Some by proper inducements, others by improper inducement. The key to successful interrogation is to design a playbook consisting of two lists – "what to do" (proper inducements) and "what not to do" (improper inducements). One list is not enough. One list gives you only half a playbook. Combining both gives you the best decision-making model to survive in the world of interrogation. Every interrogation is a series of decisions. An interrogation playbook is a decision-making model that lets you make the right call at the right time and avoid the wrong call at all times.

The problem is that you won't find definitive lists of proper and improper inducements anywhere in Canadian Law. You have to research case law and find them. You have to sift through countless case law decisions to list what specifically constitutes proper inducements and improper inducements. In a perfect world, a statute would be passed to serve as your interrogation playbook, with two chapters entitled – "What to do and what not to do." But we're living and working in an imperfect world so we have to make our own playbook.

Lesson 5

The two classifications of proper and improper inducements are based on the strength and severity of the **negative** impact. In other words, how right or wrong the motivating force is.

Lesson 6

A 100% wrong and 0% right motivating force is an **improper** inducement. Examples: violence, physical force, threat of violence, threat of more severe legal consequences or promise of leniency.

Lesson 7

A 0% wrong and 100% right motivating force is a **proper** inducement. Example: self-generated, conscience-driven force; an appeal to the conscience.

Lesson 8

A partially right and partially wrong motivating force is a **contextual** inducement. A contextual inducement becomes classified as improper or proper depending on the strength or weakness of its **negative** impact on voluntariness **and** strength or weakness to generate a false confession. There are countless examples of circumstances that qualify as "contextual inducements" that have been re-classified as "proper" and those that have been re-classified as "improper." Together, they expand the what-to-do and what-not-to-do playbook. Examples of contextual inducements are included in the rest of this series.

Lesson 9

True nature of Inducement: There's another perspective of inducement that has to be learned – primary or secondary motivator/influence. Interrogations rarely consist of just one inducement. Most interrogations consist of a series of different inducements. Example: *"The guilt of this crime will get worse. You won't find peace until you confess. Have you ever thought of professional help?"* That example appears to be one statement but it includes three inducements. Each one makes an impact. Each one may influence the suspect's decision to confess. Each inducement counts, adding up to the full context. Every inducement is a positive or negative act or statement made by a person in authority that properly or improperly motivates a person to confess. An inducement is the proper or improper driving force of a confession. An inducement can be the primary or any secondary motivator or influence that played a part in the suspect's decision-making of how to exercise free will. A contextual analysis weighs the positive and negative strength of each inducement to reach a conclusion of voluntary/reliable or forced or, false.

The true nature of an inducement is the extent of its positive or negative effect on the suspect's free will. Inner inducements produce the strongest positive effects. Outer inducements are a risk to admissibility. Some external inducements will automatically exclude a confession while others jeopardize admissibility. The secret is to make every inducement (primary and secondary) have a positive effect through internally-generated motivating forces.

Lesson 10

You can't prevent an improper inducement if you can't recognize one. Identifying an improper inducement starts with recognizing the primary characteristic of every improper inducement – an improper *quid pro quo*… an improper deal, an improper trade-off. Achieving that objective needs different perspectives of the concept of quid pro quo.

An improper inducement is defined as a *Quid Pro Quo* offer by the interrogator (PIA) *in the form of a threat or promise*.[49] The broader definition of an improper inducement is *any words or acts* made by an interrogator (PIA), that cause an accused person to believe that his/her legal status/situation relating to the investigation will *improve* or *worsen*, depending on whether or not he/she makes a statement/confession.[50]

Avoiding a quid pro quo means focusing on the definitions of and relationships between: (i) quid pro quo; (ii) threat; and (iii) promise:

(i)   Quid Pro Quo is a Latin phrase meaning: (a) a thing given or done in return for something else; (b) something in exchange for something.[51]

(ii) A threat means any act of actual violence, acts that constitute the Criminal Code definition of assault, or any words or acts that directly or indirectly imply violence.[52]

(iii) A promise means any words or acts that directly or indirectly imply a benefit.[53]

A quid pro quo inducement can be either a negative or positive driving force emerging from the PIA that compels (forces) a person to give a confession in exchange for it. Two obvious examples of quip pro quo offers are:

i.   Threatening to physically beat an offender if he refuses to confess and then the offender confesses. The offender is exchanging a confession for the *benefit* of avoiding an assault.

ii.   Promising leniency on the condition the offender confesses and then the offender confesses. The offender is exchanging the confession for the *benefit* of the specific leniency.

Lesson 11

Communication conditioning is the key to preventing improper inducements which is the strategic objective of every interrogation. Communication conditioning refers to *speech* habits and patterns which reflect our *thought* habits and patterns. Preventing quid pro quo offers needs speech hardwiring that removes any hint of

49   R. v. Oickle (2000), File No. 26535 (S.C.C.).
50   Ontario Police College, Interrogation Course, 1984.
51   Oxford Dictionary 1994, Oxford University Press, pg. 654.
52   Regina v. Fennell (1881), 7 Q.B.D. 147 (C.C.R).
53   Ibid

quid pro quo from the thought process. The temptation to offer quid pro quo deals is often strong enough without proper training. The only way to combat the temptation to resist quid pro quo offers is to practice speech that does not include quid pro quo deals. In other words, condition your interrogation with <u>proper inducement vocabulary</u>.

Conditioning your interrogation communication with <u>proper inducement vocabulary</u> is accomplished only through conscious reps – structured practice. Practicing the language of the Inducement Chart. The proper inducement list teaches you every thought and every word that you need to hardwire into your interrogation communication.

    i. Nature – the nature of the quid pro quo inducement has to be an appeal to conscience or a motivation that does not force the accused to confess against his will. The nature of the quid pro quo inducement has to keep free will fully functioning.

    ii. Source – there are three possible sources of a proper quid pro offer - PIA, PNIA, or the suspect himself (self-generated). PIA-generated quid pro quo offers are the riskiest. Self-generated inducements are the safest. If a PNIA quid pro quo is illegal, the PNIA will likely be re-classified as PIA.

    iii. Strength – Quid pro quo inducements are not created equal. They don't all have the same strength. There are strong and weak quid pro quo offers. Minimal strength, weak quid pro quo offer that are not strong enough to force an involuntary confession are an element of a proper inducement. In other words, weak quid pro quo offers that have minimal impact will likely be proper inducements

Lesson 12

<u>Source of inducement</u>: A police interrogator is only one of three possible sources of inducements. Two sources are external to the suspect (PIA and PNIA) and one is internal. Inducements by the police will be scrutinized, evaluated, and classified by a trial judge during a voir dire – an admissibility hearing <u>during</u> the trial. No voir dire will be held for persons not in authority. That doesn't mean that a PNIA can do whatever s/he wants to get a confession. It means that if a person is classified as a PNIA, the inducement is not questionable.

The primary aim of every interrogation is **self-inducement**. When the suspect is the source of the inducement, the confession will be voluntary. Conscience-generated pressure through guilt is not only a proper inducement, it's the best proper inducement. It's the preferred inducement, the natural force that brings out the truth voluntarily.

Lesson 13

<u>Threat or promise</u>: Nothing is more straightforward in criminal law than the concept of threats and promises. There's nothing complicated about it – you can't commit assault, you can't threaten bodily harm, you can't promise a light sentence, you can't threaten with harsh sentences. If you imply the consequence of physical force or harsher penalty as punishment for not confessing, the confession will be thrown out and you may be liable for threatening harm.

Confessions have to be consequence-free to be admissible. Consequences or the absence of consequences cannot be offered as quid pro quo deals in exchange for a confession.

Lesson 14

Rewards/Benefits of a confession: There's a direct relationship between *source of reward* and *confession admissibility*. Confessions produce rewards. A reward is the primary motivator for every confession. A reward is the benefit received from the confession; the advantage. The type of reward determines admissibility of a confession. The type of benefit gained by a confession determines voluntariness and reliability.

There are two possible types of rewards/benefits that may be gained from confessions: (i) internal; and (ii) external. The internal benefit of a confession is the intangible reward of *stress relief* – inner peace. The biggest reward of a confession is guilt-riddance instead of guilt-ridden. Committing crime causes cognitive dissonance[54] – internal conflict. Guilt. Cognitive dissonance is psychological pain; inner hell. The cause of cognitive dissonance is acting contrary to personal right-from-wrong moral beliefs. The stronger the belief, the worse the inner hell. The inner hell is the product of the conscience. The stronger the conscience, the higher the heat. The short-term cure is rationalization. Lies, denials, and excuses are band-aid solutions. The lasting cure for cognitive is reconciliation through confession.

Admitting the truth serves a dual purpose:

   i. It's a pain reliever. Confessions clears the conscience but, more importantly, it stops the conscience from pouring on the guilt. The internal benefit doesn't just ease pressure by one's conscience, it shuts it off.[55]

   ii. It's a catalyst for change. Admitting the truth to self is a change agent.[56] Self-truth brings on self-improvement. Self-deception doesn't.

The inner reward of a confession can't be underestimated or overstated. A conflict-free soul is what humans strive for. Getting rid of anxieties and fear brought on by the growing pressure of guilt becomes the biggest distraction and strongest obstacle from the happy life that humans struggle to achieve. The inner reward of a confession – inner peace – is the fastest, least expensive, longest-lasting, reward, and 100% natural. That's why self-generated conscience-driven confessions are voluntary and reliable – they're 100% natural. And the reward is self-generated.

External benefits are the extrinsic tangible rewards of avoiding physical or legal punishment. Extrinsic rewards are the consequence-free deal – a confession in exchange for less physical or legal punishment. External rewards are not self-generated, only internal benefit is self-generated.[57] External rewards exclude confessions.

Inner reward = confession in. Outer reward = confession thrown out.

Lesson 15

There are two driving forces that mobilize a confession: (i) an internal desire to confess (internal benefit and reward); and (ii) a desire to gain a benefit offered by an interrogator (external reward). The internal reward does *not* constitute a quid pro quo offer by the police. Consequently, it does *not* constitute an improper inducement.

---

54   Leon Festinger (1957) *A Theory of Cognitive Dissonance.* Stanford, CA: Stanford University Press.
55   Ibid.
56   Ibid.
57   Ibid.

The inner reward is a self-generated, proper inducement. External rewards *do* constitute an improper inducement because the confession was preceded by a quid pro quo offer from the police. Accordingly, the following rules emerge:

  i. A confession emerging from or driven by an internal desire to gain internal benefits/rewards is admissible because no improper inducement of threats or promise occurred.

  ii. A confession *compelled* by a desire to gain external benefits resulting from police threats or promises *may* exclude the confession because the compulsion to confess was induced. However, exclusion is not automatic because the *strength of inducement* must be at a level sufficient enough to produce an unreliable confession.

This rule gives considerable interrogation leeway regarding external inducements. Perfection is not expected but reasonableness is. In other words, some external inducements are permitted as long as they are weak and lack the strength to produce an unreliable confession. The S.C.C. did not provide a definitive list of what constitutes low level, weak external inducement. Case law research creates that list.

Lesson 16

Classifying external inducements – the 2 rules of classification: The considerable leeway regarding external inducements is not automatic. It's governed by a two-step decision-making process that the S.C.C. created in *Oickle* that classifies external inducements as proper or improper. The following are the 2 rules that decide whether an external inducement is weak enough to be a proper inducement or strong enough to be improper:

1. "The police <u>may</u> offer <u>*some kind*</u> of inducement to the suspect to obtain a confession."[58] "Few suspects will spontaneously confess to a crime. In the vast majority of cases, the police will have to somehow convince the suspect that it is in his or her best interests to confess."[59]

2. "This becomes improper only when the inducements, whether standing alone or in combination with other factors, are strong enough to raise a reasonable doubt about whether the *will of the subject has been overborne.*"[60]

Practical application/key points:

  i.   The S.C.C. was referring to <u>external inducements</u> in the above 2 rules. External inducements are not self-generated.

  ii. Rule #1 gives PIA authority to use external inducement within limits. The limit was loosely defined as "some kind" of external inducement. Rule #2 explained how to decide the limits of "some kind" of external inducement.

  iii. Rule #2 defined the distinction between improper and proper external inducements. The distinction is based on the <u>effect</u> of the external inducement and the suspect's free will.

---

58   R. v. Oickle (2000), File No. 26535 (S.C.C.) p. 19.
59   Ibid.
60   Ibid.

iv.   The relationship between the strength level of an external inducement and the suspect's free will capacity, is the deciding factor that classifies the external inducement as proper or improper.

v.   External inducements are not created equal. Some are improper. Others are not. The S.C.C. gave the police leeway by not lumping all external inducements together as being improper. External inducements will not automatically exclude a confession to a PIA because not all external inducements are improper. Some are proper.

vi.   Low level, weak external inducements are expected, tolerated, and permissible during interrogation as long as they don't cross the line between functional and non-functional free will.

vii. The deciding factor that determines what external inducements are improper and proper is the connection between: (i) strength of the external inducement; and (ii) the suspect's free will.

viii. The effect of the external inducement on the suspect's free will decides whether a confession to PIA is voluntary and reliable.

ix.   A strong external inducement overtakes a suspect's free will.

x.   A weak external inducement keeps a suspect's free will intact.

xi.   **The working condition of the suspect's free will is the top priority and main focus**. All interrogation strategy must be centered on preventing the suspect's free will from being overborne. Focus on proving beyond a reasonable doubt that the suspect's free will was functional throughout the interrogation.

xii. Free will is the freedom to choose. Full self-control over personal decisions.

xiii. External inducements will be evaluated within the context of the full interrogation to determine each one's strength level. How the external inducement fits in by itself or in conjunction with other factors is the key.

xiv. The threshold of an external inducement strength level is whether the external inducement, whether alone or combined with other factors, creates reasonable doubt about the suspect's freedom of free will. The standard of proof is not 100% certainty beyond all shadow of a doubt.

xv.   Internal self-generated inducements are safe. They do not negatively affect free will.

Lesson 17

"Explicit" offer/exception: The S.C.C. general rule for classifying improper inducements is as follows: *"An "explicit" offer by the police to promise leniency or threaten consequences in return for a confession is a "very strong" inducement and "will" exclude the confession in all cases but "exceptional circumstances."*[61]

---

61   R. v. Oickle (2000), File No. 26535 (S.C.C.) pg. 16.

Translation:

i.   "Explicit" means "definite, detailed, or concrete" – only one logical conclusion or interpretation exists.

ii. An explicit offer has *extreme* strength that unquestionably makes it an improper inducement.

iii. Exclusion is *almost automatic*. The S.C.C. opened the door for an exception in rare, undefined "exceptional circumstances." The S.C.C. didn't provide examples. This exception seems contradictory and counter-intuitive. The nature of "extreme" suggests that the exclusion would be mandatory, however, the "exceptional circumstances" gave the police even more leeway, albeit slight, leaving the door open for the remote possibility of admitting a confession that was motivated by an explicit offer of leniency or threatened violence.

Lesson 18

The S.C.C. provided only a small, limited number of explicit circumstances that constitute improper inducement. The list is common-sense and obvious:

1. **Violence**

2. **Proceedings – Advantages/disadvantages**

3. **Prolonged, intense questioning**

Lesson 19

Overbearing the suspect's will: Other than outright violence, obvious threats, and obvious advavntages/disadvantages to the proceedings, all other inducements are contextual. *Contextual* inducements are defined as comments/language/conduct that constitute an inducement but are not automatically classified as improper or proper until the inducement is evaluated within the context of the interrogation, meaning within the *entire* questioning.

The determining factor is the <u>strength of the suspect's will</u> before he confessed. Was his will *overborne* or not is the issue. If the inducements, alone, or in combination with other factors, are strong enough to raise a reasonable doubt about whether the suspect's will was overborne, the inducements are re-classified as improper – the confession is involuntary and unreliable and will be excluded. Conversely, if the inducements are weak and the accused's will is not overborne, the inducements are judged as proper and the confession will be voluntary.[62]

The accused's "will" is defined as "the mental faculty by which he/she decides on and controls his/her own actions." It refers to will-power and the ability to make decisions.[63]

Overborne means that the inducements were so strong and influential that they eliminated the suspect's free will to make intelligent decisions.

---

62   Ibid.
63   Oxford Dictionary p. 920.

Summary of Admissibility Rules:

1. If the dominant motive for making a confession is self-generated hope for a benefit, the confession is voluntary and reliable because *no* inducements occurred.[64]

2. If the hope for a benefit (advantage or avoidance of disadvantage) partially originates from a PIA, the inducement does not automatically render the confession involuntary unless the inducement diminished the suspect's will.[65]

3. The police are allowed to *convince* a suspect that it is in his/her "best interests to confess." The police *may offer some kind of inducement* to convince the suspect. The inducement cannot be improper (strong enough to overbear the suspect's will). A *proper* inducement is an acceptable interrogation practice.

Conclusion

Nothing is easier to learn and apply in all of criminal law and crime-fighting that the concept of threats or promises. Here's the short version: <u>Interrogators don't have the right to dish out punishment or control punishment.</u> Interrogators don't have the right to physically punish or legally punish. Interrogators don't have the authority to dish out consequences. Check your ego at the interrogation door. Interrogators have one job – get the truth. They are not thc moral arbiters of society. If you have control issues, find another job. You have no authority or no right to control punishment that a person suffers. And you have no control over leniency. Deciding on the consequences of the illegal act is not your job. If you want to control consequences, make the investment and become a judge. That's what I tried telling myself when I was a patrol officer. That's what I tried telling myself when I was a detective. That's the message I told college wannabe cops for twenty years. None of us is perfect. Far from it. It's easy to get pissed off at those who victimize innocent people, those who terrorize society and our loved ones; those who commit crimes against the weak and defenceless. The toughest thing I had to learn in interrogation and policing in general was this – don't take it personal, don't make it personal. No beatings, no threats of beatings, no threats to make their legal situation worse, and no promises to make the suspect's legal situation better. It's that simple. Professional bullying isn't allowed.

Be civilized, don't terrorize. Interrogations are emotional dialogues. Emotions can run high especially during an interrogation surrounding a heinous crime that has caused unspeakable human suffering but there's a line that can't be crossed. The S.C.C. has given you the green light to interrogate suspects and they've given you significant leeway along with the green light. They ask one thing – don't be a criminal. Be the good guy. Be a professional, not a street thug. They're not asking you to be a hospitable. Just don't cross the clear line that separates psychotic from professional behaviour.

---

64   R. v. Oickle (2000), File No. 26535 (S.C.C.).
65   Ibid.

Chapter 11
Force Factor #2: Oppression

This chapter includes:

    i.   Basic lessons – introductory key points.

    ii. Annotated case law – quotes from the *Oickle* judgment followed by practical translation. There are 5 passages in particular relating to Force Factor #2, "oppression," that I have entitled "Ruling #1-5."

Basic lessons

1. Oppression is defined by the S.C.C. in *Oickle* as "inhumane conditions" that would force a person to falsely confess "purely out of a desire to escape those conditions."[66]

2. Oppression is an improper inducement that motives and compels an involuntary confession.

3. In ordinary language, oppression is hell that could cause a person to attempt to escape hell by falsely confessing. Oppression causes depression; a hopelessness sets in that forces desperation, including telling the interrogator what s/he wants to hear to make the pain stop.

4. Oppressive conditions include but are not limited to, the following factors:

   - *Deprivation* of food, clothing, water, sleep, or medical attention.

   - Denying access to a lawyer (which also constitutes a Charter violation and mobilizes the sec. 24(2) Charter rule).

   - Excessively aggressive, intimidating questioning for a prolonged time period.

   - Use of non-existent evidence to deceive the suspect.[67]

5. The S.C.C. settled a case law debate originating in 1982[68], by including "oppression" in the Confessions Rule. It is now a factor that governs voluntariness. The Crown onus includes the burden of proving the *absence* of oppression. The reasons are that oppression: (i) undoubtedly has the potential to produce the stress-compliant type of false confession; and (ii) could overbear the suspect's will to the point that he/she doubts his/her own memory, believes the relentless accusations made by police, and gives an induced confession.[69]

6. The key points about oppression are the *extreme* conditions and the connection to the suspect's willpower. The extreme nature of the conditions has to be strong enough to generate a desire to escape them by means of falsely confessing.

---

66   R. v. Oickle (2000), File No. 26535 (S.C.C.).
67   Ibid.
68   R. v. Hobbins (1982) 1 S.CR 553 (S.C.C.)
69   R. v. Oickle (2000), File No. 26535 (S.C.C.).

7. Best point of reference case law: The S.C.C. referred to an Ontario Court of Appeal decision *R. v. Hoilett* (1999)[70] as a "compelling" example of oppression and oppressive environment. Although the circumstances do not constitute an *absolute definition*, it does provide interrogators with the best point of reference. Summary of the case:

- The accused was arrested and charged with sexual assault.

- He was under the influence of crack cocaine and alcohol at the time of his arrest.

- After two hours in a cell, his clothes were seized for forensic testing and he was left naked for one and a half hours. Afterward, he was given some light clothes, no underwear, and poor-fitting shoes.

- Questioning started shortly afterward. He fell asleep five times during the interrogation. He was denied requests for warmer clothes and for a tissue to wipe his nose.

- The accused admitted knowing that he understood the right to silence and admitted that the police made no explicit threat or promise. However, the accused testified at the trial that he confessed with the hope of getting warmer clothes and ending the interrogation under those conditions.

- The Ontario C.A. ruled that the circumstances constituted oppression, the confession was involuntary, and the confession was excluded.

Annotated case law (from Oickle)

Ruling #1:   *"There was much debate among the parties, interveners, and courts below over the relevance of "oppression" to the confessions rule. Oppression clearly has the potential to produce false confessions. If the police create conditions distasteful enough, it should be no surprise that the suspect would make a stress-compliant confession to escape those conditions. Alternately, oppressive circumstances could overbear the suspect's will to the point that he or she comes to doubt his or her own memory, believes the relentless accusations made by the police, and gives an induced confession."*

Translation:

i)   Oppression became part of the Confessions Rule because its consequence is relevant.

     a.   The consequence of oppression is potential for a false confession.

ii) Oppression is a distasteful environment created by the police.

     b.   An oppressive environment has the potential to cause a stress-compliant confession.

          i.   A stress-complaint confession is defined by the S.C.C. in *Oickle* as a confession that occur "when the aversive interpersonal pressures of interrogation become so intolerable that [suspects] comply in order to terminate questioning."

---

[70]   R. v. Hoilett (1999) 136 C.C.C. (3d) p. 449 (Ont. C.A.).

iii) The primary condition of an oppressive environment is <u>intolerable pressure</u>.

    a. Pressure is not created equal. Interrogations, by nature, are stressful and pressure-packed. Not all pressure is intolerable. There's a line that separates tolerable and intolerable pressure and it can't be crossed.

        i. Intolerable pressure is pressure that causes a person to reach his/her break point. Break point is the point where the suspect's free will is no longer functional. He/she can't make rational choices.

    b. Contrary to popular myth, a suspect cannot be broken down. Broken down means free will that has deteriorated past proper working condition. If the suspect cannot exercise free will, he is suffering from the effects of oppression. The break point that can't be reached is overborne free will.

vi) The main symptom of the break point where free will is no longer working right is self-doubt – doubting one's memory. Lost faith in one's memory.

    a. A chain reaction starts after the suspect doubts his memory. He believes the "relentless accusations" made by the police, believes that those accusations are true or adopts them to escape the hell created by oppression, and forces a false confession.

v) Remove "break the suspect" from your vocabulary. "Did you break Him?" "You have to break him." "We broke him." Press "delete." Breaking a suspect is improper, unlawful, illegal – it's wrong. The courts won't tolerate it. The zero tolerance is justified. An interrogation is not a medieval practice. Be civilized. Be natural. Appeal to the suspect's conscience to let the conscience naturally induce the confession.

Ruling #2: *"A compelling example of oppression comes from the Ontario Court of Appeal's recent decision in R. v. Hoilett (1999), 136 C.C.C. (3d) 449. The accused, charged with sexual assault, was arrested at 11:25 p.m. while under the influence of crack cocaine and alcohol. After two hours in a cell, two officers removed his clothes for forensic testing. He was left naked in a cold cell containing only a metal bunk to sit on. The bunk was so cold he had to stand up. One and one-half hours later, he was provided with some light clothes, but no underwear and ill-fitting shoes. Shortly thereafter, at about 3:00 a.m., he was awakened for the purpose of interviewing. In the course of the interrogation, the accused nodded off to sleep at least five times. He requested warmer clothes and a tissue to wipe his nose, both of which were refused. While he admitted knowing that he did not have to talk, and that the officers had made no explicit threats or promises, he hoped that if he talked to the police they would give him some warm clothes and cease the interrogation. Under these circumstances, it is no surprise that the Court of Appeal concluded the statement was involuntary. Under inhumane conditions, one can hardly be surprised if a suspect confesses purely out of a desire to escape those conditions."*

Translation:

i) The *Hoilett* case is a point-of-reference of what never to do.

    a. Never create inhumane conditions.

        i. What constitutes inhumane condition? The deprivations that happened in *Hoilett* are just examples. It's the point-of-reference case for inhumane conditions.

ii) Deprivation has a line that you can't cross.

    a. Oppression is excessive deprivation – deprivation that adds up to punishment through degradation.

    b. Crossing the line with excessive deprivation jeopardizes a confession if the confession is judged to be an escape from the hell the police created.

    c. Deprivation that crosses the line will cause a confession to be excluded <u>even if there were no threats or promises</u>.

    d. Add "inhumane conditions/excessive deprivation" to the Inducement Chart under Improper Inducement.

Improper Inducements

torture
violence
physical force
threats of all the above
quid pro quo deal for confession
quid pro quo offers of leniency
quid pro quo fear of prejudice
inhumane conditions/excessive deprivation

iii) Excessive deprivation has the same negative effect as threats and promises – exclusion of confession.

iv) How much deprivation will be tolerated? Commit *Hoilett* to memory. Add up the deprivation: clothes, sleep, tissues. <u>Basic needs</u>. Never deprive the suspect of basic needs. The S.C.C. is not asking you to build five-star resort conditions. Just provide the basics. It's common sense. Use common human decency. Be humane. It relates back to an earlier point – **no matter how frustrated or pissed off you are at the crime, you don't get to punish.**

v) There's enough inhumanity in this world. Don't add to it.

Ruling #3: *"Under inhumane conditions, one can hardly be surprised if a suspect confesses purely out of a desire to escape those conditions. Such a confession is not voluntary. For similar examples of oppressive circumstances, see R. v. Owen (1983), 4 C.C.C. (3d) 538 (N.S.S.C., App. Div.); R. v. Serack, [1974] 2 W.W.R. 377 (B.C.S.C.). Without trying to indicate all the factors that can create an atmosphere of oppression, such factors include depriving the suspect of food, clothing, water, sleep, or medical attention; denying access to counsel; and excessively aggressive, intimidating questioning for a prolonged period of time."*

Translation:

i) Inhumane conditions improperly induce a confession as a method of escape.

    a. A confession made to escape hell created by the police is involuntary.

ii) *Owen* and *Serack* are two more point-of-reference cases that help concretely define oppression.

iii) Add the following on the Inducement Chart under Improper Inducement: "Oppression: factors include but not limited to deprivation of: (i) basic physical needs, e.g., food, clothing, water, sleep, or medical attention; (ii) basic legal needs, i.e., denying access to a lawyer; or (iii) basic psychological needs, e.g., excessively aggressive, intimidating questioning for a prolonged time period.

    a. Basic physical needs are straightforward. I've lost count of how many times I've been asked what requests do you grant or deny? Cigarettes, alcohol, etc. The answer is "wants" versus "needs." Pain versus pleasure. Is it a basic need or not? Is it harmful to health or essential to health? If it's not listed by the S.C.C., denying it is not "excessive deprivation."

iv) The most important sentence in ruling number #3 and arguably the most important statement in all of *Oickle* is: *"excessively aggressive, intimidating questioning for a prolonged period of time"* as one factor that constitutes an atmosphere of oppression that will exclude a confession. There are five elements in this statement. All lack any concrete definition or guideline resulting in a feint, blurry, crooked line separating proper and improper inducements. All five have to be defined separately but <u>read together.</u> The five elements are: (a) questioning; (b) aggressive; (c) intimidating; (d) excessive; and (e) prolonged time.

    a. "Questioning" is not concretely defined in *Oickle*. By implication, question means the full context of the interrogation. Even though the word "questioning" suggests only one type of statement (questions), the concept of questioning includes <u>any statement</u> made by a PIA whether it's a question, comment, or answer to a suspect's question, separate or grouped into themes. This definition is derived from the combined effect of paragraphs 17 and 33 (quote in *R. v Precourt (1976)*. The word "questioning" is a slang word with a narrow, one-sided view of interrogation. Interrogations are complex dialogues that communicate more than just questions asked by the police and answered by the suspect. There's another key point – there's no difference between formal interrogation by detectives in an interrogation room and frontline communication between uniform patrol officers and suspects at crime scenes, scene of the arrest, public places, and inside a cruiser while traveling to the police station. Even though each communication is a separate questioning/interrogation, they are all connected. They affect each other. It's easy to associate questioning only with the formal interrogation but the concept of questioning also includes frontline communication. When patrol officers start the communication process, each separate questioning period forms a communication continuum where every questioning period strategically and legally affects the other.

    b. "Aggressive" is a mystifying word. When I was a detective, I was subpoenaed to testify at a voir dire regarding a confession in a trial for break, enter, and theft. The accused person was a repeat offender who I had investigated and interrogated several times. Additionally, he was an informant. The Crown Attorney called me into his office before the trial and said, "Bad news. I read your statement and notebook. Too many F-bombs. Too many inducements." He didn't even try to introduce the confession. Never understood it then, don't understand it now. Not one F-bomb was the hostile, adversarial kind. They were part of my speech pattern that I wasn't proud but it was the <u>truth</u>. I used F-bombs, just like the accused. Here's an example: The accused said, "He's fucked up" about an accomplice. I asked, "What the fuck is wrong with him?" Later, I said, "You're just as fucked up" when he explained the volume of steroids and speed he injected. I didn't shout, yell, or scream. We were familiar with each other. Not buddies but he was a recidivist who was a top-flight informant. That's how we communicated to each other for several years. I fully understand that F-bombs are not socially acceptable in certain places but how does the use of F-bombs constitute an improper inducement in this situation? "Aggressive" is an abstract concept, not concretely defined in *Oickle*, open to extreme wide-ranging interpretations. To some people, any communication above a whisper is aggressive. The problem is inconsistent subjectivity. The S.C.C. uses four words in the *Oickle* judgment, associated with aggressive – harsh, hostile, adversarial, overbearing. All are open to wide interpretations. None have concrete definitions which makes it almost impossible to predict how a stranger will define your communication skills. You're at the mercy of subjectivity, the same kind that chooses music, movies, and books – personal preferences based on worldview shaped by unique personal experiences.

c. "Intimidating" is more mystifying than aggressive. I've lost count how many times I've been told, "You look intimidating," for no good reason. My daughters have been told, "You dad's an intimidating guy," for no good reason. Here's my point – the word intimidating is a dangerous label that's hard to erase because of outright weird subjectivity that condemns without cause. The problem of <u>false labeling</u> is getting worse. If you're not smiling in your profile pic or pressing "like" a lot, you run the risk of being falsely labeled intimidating. In an interrogation room, an unjust label can jeopardize a confession and saddle you with an bad reputation simply because some people believe it's their right to slander you with labels simply for being different from them. The closest definition for "intimidating" in *Oickle* is an indirect reference at paragraph 33 – *"questioning which is oppressive and <u>calculated to overcome the freedom of will</u> of the suspect for the purpose of extracting a confession."* This definition doesn't narrow it down to specific conduct and language that isn't tolerated. There's isn't a clear line that separates intimidation from non-intimidation. We have to rely on derivative case law (in Volume 3 of this series) which will explore point-of-reference examples of what it takes for intimidation to overcome free will.

d. The word "excessively" is important because it raises the bar of what constitutes aggressive or intimidating. Reading the sentence together implies that <u>ordinary</u> aggressiveness or intimidation is not enough to exclude. The word "excessively" clearly implies an extreme. But once again, there is no concrete definition of "excessive." Defining it is a matter of sub-jectivity that will need more derivative case law research. However, the prosecution has a point of contention to argue when the issue of aggressive and intimidating is raised by the defence. This is because the question is not whether aggression or intimidation occurred, but rather what actually qualifies as aggressive or intimidating. An interrogation does not have to a social event where the best manners win the congeniality ribbon. But there is a threshold that the S.C.C. won't tolerate crossing; it's the line that separates free will *working* from free will *shut down*.

e. There's more leeway given to the police by reading *"for a prolonged period of time"* in conjunction with *"excessively aggressive, intimidating questioning."* <u>Sustained over-the-top pressure</u> is type of questioning that will be considered oppressive and an improper inducement. The implication is clear – a short, isolated incident isn't enough to qualify as oppression. Once again, there is no concrete definition of "prolonged time" because the concept of prolonged isn't measured in minutes or hours. It's measured by the <u>condition of the suspect's free will</u>.

v) What matters the most in the evaluation of the interrogation environment to determine whether it is oppressive or not is the state of the suspect's free will – is it working or not? They key to help proving that a suspect's free will is working, as time progresses during an interrogation, is ongoing evidence that the suspect is able to make choices. Prove that the suspect's decision-making is intact. Show that the suspect is continuously capable of making decisions. Test his decision-making skills.

vi) An oppressive environment takes extremes to build. It doesn't take special skill or special knowledge to prevent it from happening. It doesn't take higher education or intense training to keep an interrogation environment safe – non-oppressive. The most important factor is never losing a sense of decency and professionalism. Don't cross the line into barbarism.

Editorial: I believe that the biggest problem you will face as an interrogator is mistaken identity – passion and intensity being mistaken for aggression and intimidation. We are all different communicators. We communicate at different volume levels. We communicate with different levels of animation. Our differences are a product of nature and nurture that form true self. What a mess this world would be if we all were exact carbon copies of one person. That said, there's a growing risk of wrongful accusation – falsely labeling passionate, intense communication as being aggressive and intimidating. It's wrong. Flat-out wrong. It's a form of discrimination. Wrongfully accusing passionate, intense communicators of being aggressive and intimidating is a form of social control – to force all human behaviour into a cookie-cutter personality for one purpose – control – the never-ending desire for humans to control other humans. There is nothing worse than having to hide your true self out of fear of false labeling.

I believe that our communication style is part of our God-given calling. I believe that we are all blessed with our own personal communication style designed for one purpose – to make an impact. To make a positive impact on everyone we cross paths with. As long as we're not hurting anyone, our communication style is part of what we're called to become. That's the key – are you hurting others or making them better? Are you causing pain or relieving pain? Your God-given communication style is part of your true self and it's meant to be expressed, not suppressed. Expressing it brings out you very best. Suppress it and you'll bring out your very worst. The reason is the build-up of cognitive dissonance. The inner conflict of hiding true self becomes an internal hell that, left unchecked, will burn you up.

I believe there is no bigger interrogation problem than the blurring of the line that separates passionate, intense communication from aggression and intimidation. I believe that it's easy to get brainwashed about how we are or are not supposed to communicate. The danger works two ways. It's wrong to justify aggression and intimidation with the defence of passion and intensity. But it's just as wrong to label passion and intensity as aggression and intimidation.

Right from wrong isn't always as clear cut as the moral arbiters of society want to make it. There's a grey area. I believe one key to unraveling the mess of the grey area is open-mindedness – open your mind to see what truly is in the heart.

Ruling #4   *"A final possible source of oppressive conditions is the police use of non-existent evidence. As the discussion of false confessions, supra, revealed, this ploy is very dangerous: see Ofshe & Leo (1997a), supra, at pp. 1040-41; Ofshe & Leo (1997), supra, at p. 202. The use of false evidence is often crucial in convincing the suspect that protestations of innocence, even if true, are futile. I do not mean to suggest in any way that, standing alone, confronting the suspect with inadmissible or even fabricated evidence is necessarily grounds for excluding a statement. However, when combined with other factors, it is certainly a relevant consideration in determining on a voir dire whether a confession was voluntary."*

Translation:

i) Lying to a suspect is "very dangerous." Lying to a suspect is high-level danger.

   a. Lying about none-existent evidence is one of the biggest interrogation risks.

      i. Lying to a suspect about evidence that doesn't exist won't automatically exclude a confession but don't confuse that with tolerance because the S.C.C. sent a strong message about the danger of false evidence. The message is clear – false evidence may lead to false confession.

ii) Lying to a suspect about false evidence is <u>strong</u> reason to exclude a confession because lies strongly contribute to involuntariness.

iii) Don't take the risk. Be honest. **Honesty out, honesty in**. If you expect honesty from the suspect, be a role model. Start with yourself. **Dishonesty out, dishonesty in.** Don't forget that when you lie to a suspect, word can spread that you are a bullshitter. Here's the ramifications of having a bullshitter reputation:

   a. You may investigate the suspect again. S/he likely won't forget that you can't be trusted.

   b. Word spreads fast through the criminal community. You'll be branded as a liar.

   c. Even though the S.C.C. gave you leeway about lying, your court credibility may drop in the minds of judges if you become a serial interrogation liar.

   d. <u>It can easily lead to the worst reputation of all – that you haven't got the balls to tell the truth.</u>

Editorial: This isn't preaching. I have never understood why it's OK to lie to a suspect but get pissed off when the suspect lies to you. And not just any lie. Lying about the essence of an investigation – evidence. I've never understood why the S.C.C. didn't outright ban lying about non-existent evidence because, in my opinion, if you can look someone in the face and make-up stories about evidence, what's to stop you from actually making it up for real by planting evidence? How the hell do you trust anyone who outright lies about evidence? It makes no sense whatsoever to lie to a suspect about evidence but expect to have strong credibility as a witness in court. If a witness testified that s/he lied about the existence of evidence, the immediate question would be, "Why should I believe your testimony?"

Worst of all, think of the public when they read or hear about it in the news – "police lied to suspect during interrogation about non-existent evidence. Film at 11." How do you expect to maintain public trust when you have to resort to being a bullshitter. Finally, think of this – what other professionals do we tolerate lies from? Politicians? Doctors? Dentists? Accountants? Businesses? Teachers? Clergy? I can't think of any. We expect the truth from professionals. In conclusion, I have always found trying to teach this issue to be a waste of time. Here's what I believe from the bottom of my heart – never lie to a suspect about non-existent evidence. Do your job and find the evidence so you don't have to resort to lying about it.

Ruling #5.   *"England has also recognized the role of oppression. Section 76(8) of the Police and Criminal Evidence Act 1984 (U.K.), 1984, c. 60, states that a confession must not be the product of "oppression", which is defined to include "torture, inhuman or degrading treatment, and the use or threat of violence (whether or not amounting to torture)". The Code of Practice for the Detention, Treatment and Questioning of Persons by Police Officers goes on to offer examples of what may amount to oppression, which are similar to what I described above."*

Translation:

1. The concept of oppression is not new. It was first recognized in common law.

2. The key word relating to an oppressive environment is "degrading."

3. Regardless of what the suspect is believed to have done, s/he cannot be degraded.

4. The essence of degradation is not impoliteness or bad manners, it's inhuman treatment. Cruelty – punishment intended to lower the suspect to sub-human status.

5. Oppression is not the ordinary, <u>natural</u> pressure of a smart interrogation. It extreme, <u>unnatural</u> pressure brought on by borderline sadism.

Conclusion

<u>Clean up the environment</u>

Objective: **Build a clean environment.** One of the top interrogation priorities is to clean up the environment. A clean environment is a non-oppressive environment.

Strategy: There are 5 building blocks of a non-oppressive, clean environment.

1. Don't deprive basic needs when they are truly needed.

2. Don't cause cruel and unusual suffering.

3. Don't cross the line between tolerable and intolerable pressure.

4. Do not break down the suspect's will beyond the threshold of tolerance. Keep the suspect's free will intact. Ensure the suspect is capable of making choices.

5. Don't inflict physical pain.

Chapter 12
Force Factor #3: Operating Mind

This chapter includes basic lessons as well as annotated case law ruling from *Oickle*, relating to "Operating Mind."

Basic Lessons

The "operating mind" doctrine emerged from a series of case law decisions between 1979-1994 called the *Ward-Horvath-Whittle* case law trilogy.[71] These decisions broadened the traditional Confessions Rule by expanding the concept of voluntariness beyond threats and promises.

The operating mind concept was defined in the trilogy as circumstances <u>other than</u> threats, promises, and oppression that induce a confession, including a mental capacity that prohibits a person from deciding fully whether to confess voluntarily or not.[72] Three examples of prohibitive mental capacity and *absence of operating mind,* from the *Ward-Horvath-Whittle* case law trilogy[73] are:

i) Shock

ii) Hypnosis

iii) Complete emotional disintegration.

An "operating mind" means "a cognitive ability to make decisions." Conversely, a lack of an operating mind is the absence of decision-making abilities – often resulting in an involuntary confession. The central focus of the Crown's onus relating to the element of operating mind is the absence of *complete* emotional disintegration and the presence of a reasonable ability to make intelligence decisions, particularly about whether or not to talk to the police. As with oppression, the definition of "operating mind doctrine" suggests that an *extreme* condition is needed to "completely" disintegrate the accused's cognitive abilities.

In *Oickle*, the S.C.C. formally included the "operating mind doctrine" in the Contemporary Rule by making it one of the four elements of voluntariness. It represents a formal broadening of the concept of voluntary because "operating mind" goes beyond threats/promises and oppression. The S.C.C. defined "operating mind doctrine" as only requiring that the "accused knows what he is saying and that it may be used to his detriment."

Annotated Case Law

Ruling #1:   *"This Court recently addressed this aspect of the confessions rule in Whittle, supra, and I need not repeat that exercise here. Briefly stated, Sopinka J. explained that the operating mind requirement "does not imply a higher degree of awareness than knowledge of what the accused is saying and that he is saying it to police officers who can use it to his detriment" (p. 936).*

---

71   R. v. Whittle (1994) 2. S.CR 376 (S.C.C.); Horvath v. The Queen, [1979] 2 S.C.R. 376; Ward v. The Queen, [1979] 2 S.C.R. 30.
72   R. v. Whittle (1994) 2. S.CR 376 (S.C.C.).
73   R. v. Whittle (1994) 2. S.CR 376 (S.C.C.); Horvath v. The Queen, [1979] 2 S.C.R. 376; Ward v. The Queen, [1979] 2 S.C.R. 30.

Translation:

   i)   You don't have to prove that the suspect had a high IQ or advanced deductive reasoning.

   ii) The bar is set at <u>basic knowledge</u> – awareness of three facts:

      a. what was said (confession)

      b. who it was said to (PIA)

      c. how what was said was incriminating. What was said can be used against the suspect as evidence at a trial.

   iii) These elements are included in the formal caution. The formal caution will help prove the required basic knowledge.

   iv) Prove that the accused was not suffering from any cognitive impairment that interfered with his awareness.

Ruling #2:   *"I agree, and would simply add that, like oppression, the operating mind doctrine should not be understood as a discrete inquiry completely divorced from the rest of the confessions rule. Indeed, in his reasons in Horvath, supra, at p. 408, Spence J. perceived the operating mind doctrine as but one application of the broader principle of voluntariness: statements are inadmissible if they are "not voluntary in the ordinary English sense of the word because they were induced by other circumstances such as existed in the present case.*

    Similarly, in concluding that the confessions rule cannot be limited to the negative inquiry of whether there were any explicit threats or promises, Beetz J. offered the following explanation of the rule, at pp. 424-25:

> *Furthermore, the principle which inspires the rule remains a positive one; it is the principle of voluntariness. The principle always governs and may justify an extension of the rule to situations where involuntariness has been caused otherwise than by promises, threats, hope or fear, if it is felt that other causes are as coercive as promises or threats, hope or fear and serious enough to bring the principle into play.*

As these passages make clear, the operating mind doctrine is just one application of the general rule that involuntary confessions are inadmissible."

Translation:

   i)   The absence of an operating mind isn't the result of threats or promises.

   ii) Conversely, the absence of threats and promises doesn't guarantee an operating mind.

   iii) An operating mind is a concept separate from threats and promises but both fall under the same test of voluntariness. They are not directly connected by cause and effect but they are connected by voluntariness.

   iv) The S.C.C. unified the operating mind doctrine under the umbrella of the Contemporary Confessions Rule.

      a. The reason for unification was that the operating mind does not require a separate evaluation of the evidence from the voluntary test.

v) The Crown's burden of proving voluntariness now includes having to prove the suspect had an operating mind.

   a. Instead of the operating mind doctrine being only a defence for voluntariness, the Crown's has a bigger job by having to prove an expanded version of voluntariness.

   b. Instead of only having to prove that a confession was free from threats and promises, the prosecution has to prove the suspect had the basic awareness of what he was saying and who he was saying it to, even if he wasn't threatened or promised.

vi) Previously, a confession was ruled voluntarily if it was free from the improper inducements of threats or promises. Now, it's possible for a confession to be involuntary even if it no threats or promises occurred when the suspect's mind was not operating at the basic knowledge level that permitted him to understand the basics of what he was saying or who he was talking to or the consequences of what he was saying.

vii) Add "absence of operating mind" to the Inducement Chart under Improper Inducement.

Improper Inducements

```
torture
violence
physical force
threats of all the above
quid pro quo deal for confession
quid pro quo offers of leniency
quid pro quo fear of prejudice
inhumane conditions/excessive deprivation
absence of operating mind
```

Conclusion

Prove awareness

You have the onus to prove that the suspect has control of his mind. But your opinion about his mental capacity is inadmissible. You cannot testify that in your opinion he had an operating mind. That's a conclusion that the trial judge has to make. Build a case about the suspect's mental capacity with direct evidence and circumstantial evidence as follows:

i) The best evidence of operating mind is the full context of the interrogation. The nature of the dialogue as a whole will reveal the extent of the suspect's relevant knowledge. The key is to devote parts of the interrogation to dialogue about the relevant knowledge.

   a. The relevant knowledge means proving three relevant elements – what, who, how: (i) what he's saying (ii) who he is saying it to (iii) how it can be used against him.

ii) Teach & test. Proving knowledge is a product of teaching and learning. Proof of knowledge depends on what was learned. Measuring knowledge depending on quality of instruction and testing. Teaching and testing are the fundamentals of proving knowledge. Instruct the suspect about what you want him to know, then test him about what was learned. The basic principles of measuring knowledge are teach and test.

iii) Start with his condition. A suspect will not always be perfectly healthy at the time of an interrogation. His mind may be adversely affected by a number of physical or psychological problems. Ask questions about events <u>before</u> the interrogation, with particular attention to any event that may have caused shock or any other cognitive impairment.

     a. Progress to the Caution, both formal and informal. Contemporary case law relevant to the Caution is included in subsequent chapters. The basic premise is that the suspect must be instructed about his right to silence. Instruction is the first fundamental of proving knowledge. Follow instruction with testing. Don't ask, "What did I say?" Ask, "What does it mean?" The wrong question only tests memory. The right question tests knowledge. If he fails the test, correct him. The objective is to ensure he passes the test, not fails it.

iv) Proving knowledge doesn't require a complicated IQ test. You don't have to prove the suspect had a high IQ. Just prove he has basic awareness.

v) If the suspect shows initial awareness, it may not be enough if the interrogation goes on for a long period of time. If the interrogation is bordering on prolonged, teach and test him again. The goal is to prove that that "complete" emotional disintegration didn't occur.

vi) Like with any pressure, the pressure of interrogation is a change agent. Pressure makes an impact, either positive or negative. Some people thrive on pressure. Others crumble from it. Periodic tests during a long interrogation will help prove that cognitive decline didn't happen. A suspect's cognitive decline during a long interrogation is a potential defence.

vii) The exchange of <u>meaningful dialogue,</u> whether it's relevant or not to the crime being investigated, is powerful evidence that the suspect's cognitive condition is not in decline and that his mind is still operating.

Chapter 13
Force Factor #4: "Other" Police Trickery

This chapter explains the 4th Force Factor outlined in *Oickle*, entitled "other" police trickery. This chapter is divided into basic introductory lessons that explain the history of police trickery laws leading up to *Oickle* and the annotated case law ruling from *Oickle*.

Basic introductory lessons

i) Police trickery refers to <u>deception</u> presented to the accused during interrogation. It includes, but is not limited to, the police posing as someone who is not a police officer, e.g., lawyer, clergy, undercover officer. [74]

ii) The use of police trickery is the 4th element that governs voluntariness, which broadens the concept of voluntariness even further beyond the previous three Force Factors elements. [75]

iii) The purpose of monitoring police trickery is the specific objective of protecting the integrity of the criminal justice system. Public trust is at stake when the reputation of the criminal justice system is jeopardized. Scrutinizing police deception is intended to prevent betrayal of public trust.

iv) As a *general rule*, police trickery does not automatically render a confession involuntary and does not automatically exclude a confession. Accordingly, the S.C.C. made two classifications of police trickery:

    a. Deception that "shocks the community." This type excludes a confession because of involuntariness.

    b. Deception that does not "shock the community." This type does not exclude a confession.

        i. Examples of "shock the community" deception include:

            1. Police posing as clergy and questioning a suspect.

            2. Police posing as lawyers and questioning a suspect.

        ii. Acceptable trickery that does not "shock the community" is:

            1. The use of an <u>undercover police officer</u> (UCO), referring to a police officer posing as a person *not* in authority (except clergy and lawyer) and questioning or conversing with a suspect in a non-interrogation environment such as the police jail cells.

v) In *R. v. Rothman* (1981)[76], a landmark UCO decision, the S.C.C. made several significant rulings:

    a. A UCO in a jail cell, talking to a suspect, does not shock the community.

    b. A UCO is a person NOT in authority (P*N* IA.)

    c. A confession to the UCO was admissible.

---

74   R. v. Oickle (2000), File No. 26535 (S.C.C.).
75   Ibid.
76   R. v. Rothman (1981) 1 S.CR 640 (S.C.C.).

vi) Nine years later, the S.C.C. added to the *Rothman* ruling, in *R. v. Hebert* (1990).[77] The Rothman decision applied the Confessions Rule. The *Hebert* decision added another element to UCO investigations: sec. 24(2) Charter applies to confessions made to UCO. Confessions to UCO can violate the Charter, specifically the section 7 Charter right to silence. The circumstances in *Hebert* were as follows:

    a. The accused was arrested for robbery, was informed of the right to counsel, and was cautioned.

    b. After consulting with a lawyer, the accused invoked the sec. 7 Charter right to remain silent.

    c. Afterward, the accused was placed in a police cell with an UCO.

    d. The UCO initiated conversation.

    e. The accused made inculpatory statements to the UCO.

    f. The S.C.C. excluded the confessions under sec. 24(2) Charter, and not because use of UCO was police trickery that shocked the community – the two are separate concepts.

vii) The S.C.C., in *Oickle*, tried to clarify its position by stating that the *Hebert* decision does not change the "shock the community" classification of deception or the rules of admissibility. There remains the same two classifications of trickery. However, the *Hebert* decision goes beyond the "shock the community" rule that relates to voluntariness by adding the application of the sec 24(2) Charter rule.

Annotated Case Law

Ruling #1:   *"A final consideration in determining whether a confession is voluntary or not is the police use of trickery to obtain a confession. Unlike the previous three headings, this doctrine is a distinct inquiry. While it is still related to voluntariness, its more specific objective is maintaining the integrity of the criminal justice system. Lamer J.'s concurrence in Rothman, supra, introduced this inquiry. In that case, the Court admitted a suspect's statement to an undercover police officer who had been placed in a cell with the accused. In concurring reasons, Lamer J. emphasized that reliability was not the only concern of the confessions rule; otherwise the rule would not be concerned with whether the inducement was given by a person in authority. He summarized the correct approach at p. 691:*

> *[A] statement before being left to the trier of fact for consideration of its probative value should be the object of a voir dire in order to determine, not whether the statement is or is not reliable, but whether the authorities have done or said anything that could have induced the accused to make a statement which was or might be untrue. It is of the utmost importance to keep in mind that the inquiry is not concerned with reliability but with the authorities' conduct as regards reliability."*

Translation:

i)   Police trickery is not a new concept. It was the issue in the *Rothman* decision in 1981.

ii) The S.C.C. added police trickery as the 4th element of the definition of voluntary.

---

77   R. v. Hebert (1990) 2 S.CR 151 (S.C.C.).

a. However, this element requires a separate voir dire to determine whether the confession was true or false.

Ruling #2: *"Lamer J. was also quick to point out that courts should be wary not to unduly limit police discretion (at p. 697):*

> *[T]he investigation of crime and the detection of criminals is not a game to be governed by the Marquess of Queensbury rules. The authorities, in dealing with shrewd and often sophisticated criminals, must sometimes of necessity resort to tricks or other forms of deceit and should not through the rule be hampered in their work. What should be repressed vigorously is conduct on their part that shocks the community. [Emphasis added.]*

As examples of what might "shock the community", Lamer J. suggested a police officer pretending to be a chaplain or a legal aid lawyer, or injecting truth serum into a diabetic under the pretense that it was insulin. Lamer J.'s discussion on this point was adopted by the Court in Collins, supra, at pp. 286-87; see also R. v. Clot (1982), 69 C.C.C. (2d) 349 (Que. Sup. Ct.)."

Translation:

i)   The S.C.C. gave the police discretion to use some deceptive tactics.

   a.   This leeway is not absolute. It is limited – to deceptive tactics that do not "shock the community.

      i.   Shocking the community is defined as police deception that adversely affects the reputation of the criminal justice system and jeopardizes public trust and faith in the system.

ii) Police deception that shocks the community constitutes an improper inducement that excludes a confession because of involuntariness.

iii) Three example of police deception that shocks the community are posing as clergy, a lawyer, or injecting truth serum to get a confession.

iv) Add "Police deception that shocks the community, e.g., posing as clergy, lawyer, injecting truth serum" to the Inducement Chart under Improper Inducement.

Improper Inducements

torture
violence
physical force
threats of all the above
quid pro quo deal for confession
quid pro quo offers of leniency
quid pro quo fear of prejudice
inhumane conditions/excessive deprivation
absence of operating mind
Police deception that shocks the community, e.g., posing as clergy, lawyer, injecting truth serum

Ruling #3.　　*"In Hebert, supra, this Court overruled the result in Rothman based on the Charter's right to silence. However, I do not believe that this renders the "shocks the community" rule redundant. There may be situations in which police trickery, though neither violating the right to silence nor undermining voluntariness per se, is so appalling as to shock the community. I therefore believe that the test enunciated by Lamer J. in Rothman, and adopted by the Court in Collins, is still an important part of the confessions rule."*

Translation:

i)　UCOs are still acceptable deceptive tactics to get a confession if the right to silence is not violated.

ii)　UCOs remain PNIA.

iii)　The right to silence does not apply if the suspect is not under arrest.

　　　a.　If the UCO talks to the suspect in public and reasonable grounds do not exist to arrest, the UCO is a PNIA. If the suspect confesses, the confession is admissible under the Confessions Rule. The Charter doesn't apply when the suspect legitimately and legally is not in custody.

iv)　If the suspect is in custody and initiates conversation with the UCO, the right to silence may be considered waived.

v)　If the suspect is in custody and has not invoked his right to silence, a confession to a UCO is subject only to the Confessions Rule and will be admissible.

Conclusion

<u>Be up front, don't be underhanded</u>

The S.C.C. has given the police creative leeway to get the truth from a suspect. The UCO strategy was the only deceptive strategy allowed in *Oickle*. Other than UCO, don't try using schemes that involve acting in professions that are afforded legitimate and legal confidentiality. Bona fide communication with lawyers, clergy, doctors, psychiatrists is protected by professional standards of privileged communication – privacy. If a profession or relationship does not include that level of privacy, the implication is that it's acceptable to pose as that person to get a confession from the suspect. In other words, posing as a PNIA who is not afforded privileged communications seems to be acceptable.

Chapter 14
S.C.C. *Oickle* Summary of the Contemporary Confessions Rule

At the conclusion of the rulings regarding the four elements of the Contemporary Confessions Rule, the S.C.C. wrote a summary that paints the boundaries for interrogations.

Annotated case law

Ruling #1:   *"While the foregoing might suggest that the confessions rule involves a panoply of different considerations and tests, in reality the basic idea is quite simple. First of all, because of the criminal justice system's overriding concern not to convict the innocent, a confession will not be admissible if it is made under circumstances that raise a reasonable doubt as to voluntariness. Both the traditional, narrow Ibrahim rule and the oppression doctrine recognize this danger. If the police interrogators subject the suspect to utterly intolerable conditions, or if they offer inducements strong enough to produce an unreliable confession, the trial judge should exclude it. Between these two extremes, oppressive conditions and inducements can operate together to exclude confessions. Trial judges must be alert to the entire circumstances surrounding a confession in making this decision."*

Translation:

i) Never ignore simplicity.

   a. Simplicity #1: Despite the complexities of the Contemporary Confessions Rule, it all boils down to one simple principle – innocent people cannot ever be convicted. The prevention of wrongful conviction is the top priority. To achieve this objective, reasonable doubt about voluntariness will exclude a confession. To get a confession admitted, prove its voluntariness beyond reasonable doubt. That's why the bar is raised. The bar will never be lowered under any circumstances.

   b. Simplicity #2: There's zero tolerance for <u>extreme</u> wrongs being committed during the interrogation.

      i. Zero tolerance for intolerable conditions.

      ii. Zero tolerance for strong improper inducements.

   c. Simplicity #3: Extreme doesn't have to be one act. Extreme can be the cumulative effect of oppressive conditions and improper external inducements. Each one counts. Each one adds up. If the final count equals an extreme that crosses the line, the confession will be excluded.

   d. Simplicity #4: Every word, every act matters. The entire context of the interrogation has to be taken into consideration not just the presence or absence of isolated incidents but because it doesn't take just one extreme wrong to exclude a confession. Lesser wrongs can add up to extreme wrong. In other words, the absence of one extreme wrong won't admit a confession. The absence of cumulative wrongs will admit the confession.

Ruling #2. *"The doctrines of oppression and inducements are primarily concerned with reliability. However, as the operating mind doctrine and Lamer J.'s concurrence in Rothman, supra, both demonstrate, the confessions rule also extends to protect a broader conception of voluntariness "that focuses on the protection of the accused's rights and fairness in the criminal process": J. Sopinka, S. N. Lederman and A. W. Bryant, The Law of Evidence in Canada (2nd ed. 1999), at p. 339. Voluntariness is the touchstone of the confessions rule. Whether the concern is threats or promises, the lack of an operating mind, or police trickery that unfairly denies the accused's right to silence, this Court's jurisprudence has consistently protected the accused from having involuntary confessions introduced into evidence. If a confession is involuntary for any of these reasons, it is inadmissible."*

Translation:

i)   Force Factors are created equal.

ii) Even though there's a 2x2 split, where two elements are related to reliable and two are related to voluntariness, all it takes is one Force Factor to raise a reasonable doubt of involuntariness.

iii) The police have to prevent all four Force Factors from coming into play.

iv) Voluntariness is still the benchmark of confession admissibility – the "touchstone."

Ruling #3. *"Wigmore perhaps summed up the point best when he said that voluntariness is "shorthand for a complex of values": Wigmore on Evidence (Chadbourn rev. 1970), vol. 3, § 826, at p. 351. I also agree with Warren C.J. of the United States Supreme Court, who made a similar point in Blackburn v. Alabama, 361 U.S. 199 (1960), at p. 207:*

> *[N]either the likelihood that the confession is untrue nor the preservation of the individual's freedom of will is the sole interest at stake. As we said just last Term, "The abhorrence of society to the use of involuntary confessions . . . also turns on the deep-rooted feeling that the police must obey the law while enforcing the law; that in the end life and liberty can be as much endangered from illegal methods used to convict those thought to be criminals as from the actual criminals themselves." . . . Thus a complex of values underlies the stricture against use by the state of confessions which, by way of convenient shorthand, this Court terms involuntary, and the role played by each in any situation varies according to the particular circumstances of the case.*

See Hebert, supra. While the "complex of values" relevant to voluntariness in Canada is obviously not identical to that in the United States, I agree with Warren C.J. that "voluntariness" is a useful term to describe the various rationales underlying the confessions rule that I have addressed above."

Translation:

i)   Criminal acts won't be tolerated to convict criminals.

    a.   The police are not above the law.

    b.   A confession can't be obtained "at any cost."

ii) The repetitiveness of this message shows that the S.C.C. is concerned about the temptation for the police to go overboard in the interrogation room. The same message has been communicated in as many different ways as possible – democracy won't tolerate a police state where the police can ignore laws.

Ruling #4: *"Again, I would also like to emphasize that the analysis under the confessions rule must be a contextual one. In the past, courts have excluded confessions made as a result of relatively minor inducements. At the same time, the law ignored intolerable police conduct if it did not give rise to an "inducement" as it was understood by the narrow Ibrahim formulation. Both results are incorrect. Instead, a court should strive to understand the circumstances surrounding the confession and ask if it gives rise to a reasonable doubt as to the confession's voluntariness, taking into account all the aspects of the rule discussed above. Therefore a relatively minor inducement, such as a tissue to wipe one's nose and warmer clothes, may amount to an impermissible inducement if the suspect is deprived of sleep, heat, and clothes for several hours in the middle of the night during an interrogation: see Hoilett, supra. On the other hand, where the suspect is treated properly, it will take a stronger inducement to render the confession involuntary. If a trial court properly considers all the relevant circumstances, then a finding regarding voluntariness is essentially a factual one, and should only be overturned for "some palpable and overriding error which affected [the trial judge's] assessment of the facts": Schwartz v. Canada, [1996] 1 S.C.R. 254, at p. 279 (quoting Stein v. The Ship "Kathy K", [1976] 2 S.C.R. 802, at p. 808) (emphasis in Schwartz)."*

Translation:

i. The S.C.C. recognized that the system has not been a model of high performance. The S.C.C. acknowledged ass-backward decisions – thrown out confessions that should have been called safe and visa-versa.

ii. This ruling is a strong message of reform sent to the CJS to get its act together. The message is a directive to raise the performance level by striking the balance to determine what truly matters, what doesn't matter, and then ruling accordingly.

iii. This passage is a report card on the past performance of the system – look at interrogation with a wide lens. See the big picture, not just one piece of it.

Editorial: The critics who slam police interrogation methods need to be reminded of the above quote. Ruling #4 implies a systemic failure, not just a police failure. The critics need to be reminded that the courts also misinterpreted the laws by throwing out confessions that should not have been thrown out and allowing confessions that should not have been allowed. That's not a trivial problem. I can't think of bigger problem. Even though the S.C.C. didn't provide stats or data about how bad the problem was, the S.C.C. quote is enough to shake trust and faith in the entire system. Why did it take until the year 2000 to send this message? Why did we have to wait until the 21st century for reform? Is the post-Oickle system working better?

Ruling #5:   *"In summary, there were several aspects of the police's interrogation of the respondent that could potentially be relevant to the voluntariness of his confessions. These include the comments regarding Ms. Kilcup; the suggestions that "it would be better" for the respondent to confess; and the exaggeration of the polygraph's accuracy. These are certainly relevant considerations when determining voluntariness. However, I agree with the trial judge that neither standing alone, nor in combination with each other and the rest of the circumstances surrounding the respondent's confessions, do these factors raise a reasonable doubt about the voluntariness of the respondent's confessions. The respondent was never mistreated, he was questioned in an extremely friendly, benign tone, and he was not offered any inducements strong enough to raise a reasonable doubt as to voluntariness in the absence of any mistreatment or oppression. As I find no error in the trial judge's reasons, the Court of Appeal should not have disturbed her findings."*

Translation:

i)   The *Oickle* interrogation was non-oppressive. This case is a "point-of-reference model" of what constitutes a proper interrogation environment.

   a.   The entire context of the *Oickle* interrogation showed no inducement that, by itself or combined with other inducement, was strong enough to be deemed improper. No improper inducements were strong enough to raise a reasonable doubt about voluntariness. Instead, the context showed a proper connection between inducements – how they linked together to induce a proper self-generated confession. The key is how the inducements added up. In this case, they added up properly.

ii) The *Oickle* confession was deemed the truth because there was no evidence introduced of the confession potentially being false. Nothing happened during this interrogation that could have been construed as a cause of a false confession. There's a direct relationship between proper inducements and a true confession. When the totality of the inducements add up to being proper, there's no suspicion or conclusion of a false confession.

Chapter 15
False Confessions

You can't prevent what is not understood. One goal of the Confessions Rule is to *prevent a false confession*. The concept of "false" is a psychological phenomenon that, although uncommon, must be acknowledged and included at the forefront of interrogation laws.

The S.C.C., in *R. v. Oickle* (2000),[78] formally acknowledged the potential of false confessions by recognizing the growing body of academic literature emerging from research that changed the perspective of false confessions. False confessions are no longer considered the improbabilities, as they once were.

Why would a rationale human risk going to jail by confessing to a crime that s/he didn't commit? In 1981, research conducted with mock juries showed that most people agree that the concept of false confession doesn't make sense. The study showed a general skeptical, jaded view about the potential of false confessions – people find it difficult to believe that someone would falsely confess to a crime. Most people believe it to be counterintuitive that an innocent person would confess to a crime he/she did not commit.[79] New research shows otherwise. There have been "hundreds" of cases of false confessions that show it's a problem that needs to be addressed and prevented. The 1981 research led to False Confession Taxonomy that includes five kinds of false confessions. This model explains why false confessions happen. The Contemporary Confessions Rule, in an effort to avoid miscarriages of justice, recognizes which interrogation techniques commonly produce false confessions.

False Confession Taxonomy

i)   Voluntary

ii) Stress-compliant

iii) Coerced-compliant

iv) Non-coerced-persuaded

v)   Coerced-persuaded

The first type (voluntary) is *not* the product of improper interrogation the other 4 are.

i) *Voluntary*: This type of false confession is 100% self-generated without any police interrogation or police prompting whatsoever. The suspect chooses to falsely confess without any police involvement. Because the choice to falsely confess in this manner is not the result of police interrogation, this type of false confession is "not a concern to the courts."

ii) *Stress-Compliant*: This type of false confession occurs when the aversive interpersonal pressures of interrogation become so intolerable that the suspect complies in order to terminate questioning. These types of false confessions are elicited by exceptionally strong use of aversive stressors typically present in interrogation and given knowingly in order to escape the punishing experience of interrogation. Another feature of this type of false confession is confronting the suspect with fabricated evidence to convince the suspect that his claims of innocence are futile.

---

78   R. v. Oickle (2000), File No. 26535 (S.C.C.).
79   S. M. Kassin and L. S. Wrightsman, "Coerced Confessions, Judicial Instructions, and Mock Juror Verdicts" (1981), 11 *J. Applied Soc. Psychol.* 489; as in *Oickle*.

iii) Coerced-compliant: The majority of false confessions are of this type. They are the product of coercive influence techniques (e.g., threats and promises).

iv) Non-coerced-persuaded: This type of false confession is produced by tactics that cause an innocent person to become confused, doubt his memory, be temporarily persuaded of his guilt and confess to a crime he did not commit. Again, the use of fabricated evidence can convince an innocent person of false guilt.

v) Coerced-persuaded: This type of confession combines elements from types 2-4. [80]

The Court made the following six conclusions about false confessions:

1. Compliant personalities combined with personal histories and special characteristics or situations can trigger false confessions when persuaded by interrogative suggestion.

2. The strength of mind and will of the accused, the influence of custody or its surroundings and the effects of questions or of conversations are all factors that must be considered when a court endeavors to determine voluntariness of a confession.

3. Nonexistent evidence poses a risk. Presenting fabricated evidence to a suspect is dangerous. It has the potential either to persuade a susceptible person or convince him that his claims of innocence are wrong.

4. False confessions are rarely the product of proper interrogations. Instead, they almost always involve shoddy police practice and/or police criminality.

5. Eliciting a false confession requires strong incentive, intense pressure, and prolonged questioning.

6. *"Only under the <u>rarest of circumstances</u> do an interrogator's ploys persuade an innocent suspect that he is in fact guilty."*[81] This direct S.C.C. quote is a reminder that false confessions are <u>uncommon</u>. They happen in extraordinary circumstances when extreme wrongs build an extremely oppressive environment.

Key points – practical strategy

1. **Corroborate a confession.** It's easy to wrap up an investigation the moment the suspect signs the confession. A signed confession is a double-edged sword – it's the most important evidence in any case but it can build complacency. It's easy to forget there's more work to do, including corroborating the confession. Proving a true confession is facilitated by supporting evidence. Attempt to corroborate as many points of the confession as possible to prove whether a confession is true or false. The more points corroborated helps prove a confession is the truth. A 100% unsubstantiated confession is a problem – specifically, a candidate for a false confession.

2. **Concrete information.** Like most lies, false confessions will likely be vague. They will lack specifics. The more concrete information helps prove it's the truth. Quantity of concrete information in a confession is excellent corroboration.

---

80   R. J. Ofshe and R. A. Leo, "The Social Psychology of Police Interrogation: The Theory and Classification of True and False Confessions" (1997), *16 Stud. L. Pol. & Soc.* 189; as referenced and explained in *Oickle*.
81   R. v. Oickle (2000), File No. 26535 (S.C.C.).

3. **Isolated knowledge.** Confessions that include details of the crime that only the suspect could have known help prove the confession is true, not false. Isolated knowledge is knowledge of a crime's specific details that were not public knowledge, not wide-spread. Isolated knowledge that only the suspect could have had is excellent corroboration.

4. **Ask for a reason why the suspect confessed.** After a suspect confesses, make it a habit to ask why s/he confessed. Record the reason. The reason is not 100% proof that a confession is true but it's circumstantial evidence that helps prove the confession is true. It's another piece of the puzzle, and it's another piece of circumstantial evidence that adds up while you build a context.

5. **Ask who else the susupect confessed to.** After a suspect confess, it's very easy to overlook the likelihood that s/he confessed to a lot of people before confessing to you. One of the most overlooked question following a confession is: "Who else have you told, who have you confessed to?" The answer will build your case because confessions to PNIA are automatically admissible. Confessions to PNIA are part of plan B in case the confession made to you is thrown out. And confessions to PNIA help prove the confession he made to you is true, not false.

Chapter 16
Caution and Videotape: Two Supplements of Proving Voluntary

Can't script because you can't predict. It's impossible to script an interrogation because it's impossible to predict every response to your questions/comments. The potential circumstances of an interrogation and confession are limitless. No two interrogations in their entire context are exactly alike – there will always be some difference that makes each interrogation and confession unique. That's why you can't perfectly fit *Oickle* into any other case either as a how-to model or as an evaluation case at a trial for admissibility. *Oickle* only serves as a comparison case of what worked in the specific circumstances (the context) of *Oickle*.

The key in every interrogation is to prevent improper inducements strong enough to raise a reasonable doubt about voluntariness. Training is needed to be able to make rapid-fire "right" calls during an interrogation to prevent improper inducements, but there are two supplements that may help prove voluntariness: (i) the "caution", and; (ii) videotape.

The caution and videotape are the final topics covered in *Oickle* that are relevant to the Contemporary Confessions Rule. This chapter explains only the basics – only what *Oickle* ruled about them. A number of post-*Oickle* case law explanations regarding caution and videotape are included in subsequent volumes of this book series.

Caution

The "caution" rules add to the mess and confusion of interrogation laws. The caution is a perfect example of how Canadian interrogation laws are stuck in the past, using mechanical language from a century ago that has little relevance to how we communicate today. The formal caution is a paragraph written in ancient language that offenders are expected to understand in the blink of an eye but as we'll discover in this book series, in-depth study is required to understand it.

Study the caution laws carefully and you'll see a lot that doesn't make sense, starting with the fact that it communicates the right to silence but the phrase "right to silence" isn't anywhere to be found in the formal caution or even the name of the caution. How are you expected to instruct the suspect that he has the right to remain silent in language from a past era that doesn't get to the point and doesn't even include the main message – that the suspect has the right to remain silent?

During two decades of teaching Canadian college wannabe police officers who have been brought up on American Hollywood cops telling American bad guys, "You have the right to remain silent," the most confounding topic I taught was the full meaning of the caution. Try explaining to a college student that Canadian police:

i. don't say that phrase even though that's the message they're trying to send, and;

ii. don't even have to say the "caution" at all because no law makes it mandatory.

What should be a five minute lesson turns into a full course. There's no rational need for the current complexity of the caution. We can't even get the name straight – some of us call it the "caution" while others call it the "warning." The bottom line is the purpose – it's to teach a suspect, instruct him/her of basic knowledge – make them aware of the following simple points:

i)   You don't have to talk to the police.

ii) You have the right to remain silent during police questioning.

iii) You can't be forced to answer any police questions about the crime.

iv) If you do talk to the police, it's your choice. You have to consent to it.

v)   If you decide to talk to the police, whatever you say may be self-incriminating evidence. The prosecution may be able to use what you say against you.

Definition of caution:

There are two types of cautions – informal and formal. A formal caution has versions that may differ from one police jurisdiction to another but they're all intended to communicate the same message. The one that I was taught and used for 15 years in policing and then taught college students for another 20 years is: *"Do you wish to say anything in answer to the charge? You are not obliged to say anything unless you wish to do so, but whatever you say may be given as evidence."* An informal caution is a warning, given in ordinary language, that includes the same ingredients as the formal caution but without the formality.

If you search *Oickle* for "caution" you will get zero matches; the word is not used. The only reference to the caution is in Ruling #1 below, where "police warning" is used. (From the moment I learned it at police college to the day I left policing, I never heard the phrase "police warning." Not once. Not in a police station, not in court. We were taught and used the word "caution" exclusively. And, I still use caution throughout this book series because it's easier for teaching and learning.) The bottom line is that *Oickle* remained silent on "caution laws." The S.C.C. said nothing about what to do or not to do.

The following is an annotated case law and translation (Basic Caution 101) which will serve as a foundation for post-*Oickle* case law explanations found in future volumes of this book series.

Annotated case law

Ruling #1   *"Constable Bogle took over the interrogation at 9:52 p.m., after giving the respondent the <u>secondary police warning</u>. Constable Bogle questioned the respondent until about 11:00 p.m., at which time the respondent confessed to setting seven of the eight fires. He denied any involvement in the fire in his father's van. At this time, Constable Bogle left the room, and the respondent was seen crying with his head in his hands. Constable Bogle returned with Corporal Deveau, and took a written statement. The respondent's Charter rights and the **<u>police warning were on the statement,</u>** and were acknowledged by the respondent. The **<u>police warning</u>** stated that "[y]ou need not say anything. You have nothing to hope from any promise or favour and nothing to fear from any threat whether or not you do say anything. Anything you do say may be used as evidence."** The statement concluded at 1:10 a.m. on April 27. After the police attended to various administrative tasks, the respondent was placed in a cell to sleep at 2:45 a.m. At 6:00 a.m., Corporal Deveau* *noticed that the respondent was awake and asked whether he would agree to a re-enactment. On the tape of the re-enactment, the respondent was given a Charter warning, the <u>secondary warning</u>, and was advised that he could stop the re-enactment at any time. The police drove the respondent around Waterville to the various fire scenes, where he described how he had set each fire. The respondent was charged with seven counts of arson.*

Translation:

i) The accused was cautioned and informed of his right to counsel after he confessed.

ii) The caution was called the "police warning." Shortly afterward, in the decision, the S.C.C. used the phrase "Charter warning" in reference to the right to counsel. Needless confusion. Referring to both as "warnings" adds to the confusion about their meaning. The right to counsel is an instruction, not a warning. The same applies with the caution. The caution is an instruction – what the suspect needs to know in order to make <u>informed decisions</u>. The key to both the right to counsel and the caution is to teach the suspect so that he is capable of making <u>informed decisions</u>. Using "warning" confuses the issue because:

    a. It implies a danger exists. I understand that the suspect is in danger of self-incrimination and in danger of receiving no legal advice if he waives the right to counsel, but both the caution and right to counsel are founded on the principle of decision-making, not danger. Proper delivery of instruction makes the consequences clear. The word "warning" detracts from the purpose of instruction – which is to ensure that the suspect can exercise his free will intelligently.

    b. It also means a "don't-do-it-again break" to the average citizen – a police decision to not charge an offender. Why use a word that can easily be confused with a police decision to not charge when the opposite is what's actually happening?

iii) The "secondary warning" adds to the confusion. In this case, it amounted to an instruction that the suspect could stop the crime re-enactment. Essentially, he was instructed that he could withdraw consent. The consent instructions found in case law have the same characteristics as the caution and secondary caution. In my opinion, there needs to be reform to condense all of them into a common instruction that applies to any circumstance involving the suspect's need to make an informed decision.

iv) The S.C.C. made no clear ruling about the connection between the caution and voluntariness. The implication is that the caution was one factor but we are not told the impact that the caution had on each inducement separately or in combination with each other. The extent of the caution's impact given the total context of the interrogation is important to clarify the mystery about what the caution means to minor improper inducements. The absence of a clear ruling leaves the mystery unsolved. We don't know what role the caution had on the minor improper inducements and the conclusion of voluntariness.

v) Don't fall in the trap of believing that the caution clears the way to say or do whatever you want during an interrogation. The caution is not a green light that will justify or cancel out serious improper inducements. The caution is merely one factor that helps prove that the suspect knew what he was saying, to who, and the consequences of saying it. The caution is only a supplement that assists in proving voluntariness but it won't automatically prove voluntariness.

Key points:

The key points of the caution are as follows:

i) The caution is a formal warning to the suspect that he has <u>no obligation</u> to speak to the <u>police</u> or answer police questions but his answers may become <u>admissible self-incriminating evidence</u>.

ii) In addition to being a warning, the caution teaches the suspect the basic knowledge of what he needs to knows before an interrogation – the caution communicates the ground rules.

iii) The caution is not a "demand" (similar to a breath demand) to answer questions. The decision to speak to the police must be by consent. The caution informs the suspect that s/he can't be forced to answer police questioning and that there are no legal consequences for refusing to answer police questions.

iv) The caution formally instructs the suspect that s/he has the <u>right to remain silent</u> but the phrase "right to remain silent" is not used in the formal caution and it's not included in the title "caution."

v) Failing to read the caution is not a Charter violation because the Charter does not impose an obligation to caution an adult suspect. It is not mandatory under statute law or case law for adult offenders. The caution is discretionary. It is a supplement, a potential benefit to the prosecution that <u>helps</u> prove voluntariness.

vi) Failure to caution a suspect does not guarantee confession exclusion and reading the caution does not guarantee admission of a confession. The caution is one factor that helps prove voluntary but it is not a definitive factor.

vii) The caution will help classify minor improper inducements as too weak to raise a reasonable doubt of voluntariness. The caution will not negate a major improper inducement however, it may help classify minor improper inducements as proper inducements.

History of the caution:

The caution started with the Judges Rules – interrogation <u>guidelines</u> written in England in 1912. These guidelines included recommendations that a person in custody <u>should not</u> be interrogated with first being cautioned and that the formal caution should be used instead of informal. The Rules were not law and have never been made statutory law in Canada. The caution was never included as a mandatory obligation in the Criminal Code, Canada Evidence Act, Charter, or any other statute.

Prior to *Oickle*, the last landmark case law decision that governed the caution was *Boudreau v. The King* (1949).[82] The following elements of the *"Boudreau" Doctrine"* emerged from that case:[83]

i) The fundamental issue governing the admissibility of confessions is voluntariness, not the caution.

ii) The failure to caution does not result in automatic exclusion of a confession at a trial.

---

82   Boudreau v. The King (1949) CR 427 (S.C.C.).
83   R. v. Dalzell (2003) CanLII 49355 (ON S.C.)

iii) The absence of a caution does not automatically qualify a confession as involuntary.

iv) The "mere fact" that the caution is read to an accused prior to a confession does not guarantee admissibility. A proper caution does not automatically qualify a confession as voluntary.

v) The presence or absence of a caution is *one* factor that is considered in the determination of voluntariness. In many cases, it is an important factor, but not the only factor.

vi) An arrest or detention, or the formation of a *reasonable grounds belief* is the catalyst for the caution. The necessity for a caution is connected to the level of *belief*:

   a. A belief based on reasonable grounds mobilizes the need for a caution.

   b. Conversely, no caution is needed when the belief is below reasonable grounds (i.e., mere suspicion).

The governing rule about who and when to caution emerged from the following statement in Boudreau: *"... when the police or others in authority have either arrested the accused or made up their minds that he is the party whom they will prosecute, then before being questioned he should be cautioned or warned in a manner that will explain his position."*

In 2003, R.v Dalzell created the Contemporary Caution Rule. This case and related case law will be explained in subsequent volumes of this book series. The Youth Criminal Justice Act includes statutory provisions governing cautioning young offenders.

Editorial: The caution is antiquated. It's an example of ancient laws and language, shaped over a century ago and re-shaped in a futile attempt to fit into 21st century communication. The formal caution was written, long before the Charter. Instead of re-writing the caution when the Charter was enacted, we insisted on keeping stodgy language from an era that has long since disappeared. To make matters worse, section 7 Charter includes the "right to silence" but the phrase is nowhere to be found in sec. 7 Charter. The formal caution is counter-productive, mechanical and needs to be humanized, to eliminate every confusing word or phrase.. It does not speak the language of modern 21st century multi-cultural Canada. The formal caution needs to be informalized, with discretion to customize it to the level of individual understanding.

Another reason for formal caution reform is that the caution connects the Charter with the Confessions Rule. It links the right to voluntariness. Even though they are separate concepts, they are tied together – the right to remain silent is part of the decision-making process that decides voluntariness but they are separate laws and rule.

The S.C.C. in Oickle didn't help. The S.C.C. had the chance to modernize the formal caution and bring it into the 21st century but they never mentioned the word caution in the entire judgment. And there has to be a decision about making the caution mandatory and what impact it actually has. The police, judges, suspects, and defence lawyers all need to know exactly what effect the caution has on minor improper inducements. The current system is set up for failure because there is no clear direction.

Videotaping

Adding to the confusion is the question of whether there is a mandatory obligation for the police to videotape interrogations, the S.C.C., in *Oickle*, strongly recommended electronic recording but did not make it mandatory.

Annotated case law

Ruling #1:   *"Before turning to how the confessions rule responds to these dangers, I would like to comment briefly on the growing practice of recording police interrogations, preferably by videotape. As pointed out by J. J. Furedy and J. Liss in "Countering Confessions Induced by the Polygraph: Of Confessionals and Psychological Rubber Hoses" (1986), 29 Crim. L.Q. 91, at p. 104, even if "notes were accurate concerning the content of what was said . . ., the notes cannot reflect the tone of what was said and any body language that may have been employed" (emphasis in original). White, supra, at pp. 153-54, similarly offers four reasons why videotaping is important:*

> *First, it provides a means by which courts can monitor interrogation practices and thereby enforce the other safeguards. Second, it deters the police from employing interrogation methods likely to lead to untrustworthy confessions. Third, it enables courts to make more informed judgments about whether interrogation practices were likely to lead to an untrustworthy confession. Finally, mandating this safeguard accords with sound public policy because the safeguard will have additional salutary effects besides reducing untrustworthy confessions, including more net benefits for law enforcement."*

Translation:

i) First, the S.C.C. made the case as to why electronic recording is needed. Heading the list is the fact that police notes are deficient because they fail to prove the nature and effect of non-verbal communication – tone and body language.

ii) There are four more benefits of electronically recorded interrogations:

   a. Precise evaluation. Videotaping is a re-enactment of the interrogation, allowing the courts to evaluate the full context. Notebooks can't re-create the full context because non-verbal communication is missing.

   b. Prevention of major improper inducements.

   c. Allows the court to make fully informed decisions about voluntariness and reliability.

   d. Protects law enforcement from false allegations.

iii) Not one negative was mentioned about electronic videotaping. In other words, there's no comparison – videotape beats notes.

Ruling #2:   *"This is not to suggest that non-recorded interrogations are inherently suspect; it is simply to make the obvious point that when a recording is made, it can greatly assist the trier of fact in assessing the confession."*

Translation:

i.   Despite the superiority of electronically-recorded interrogations, they are not mandatory. But if you do videotape a full interrogation, it's a bonus.

ii. Failure to record an interrogation doesn't negatively impact voluntariness.

iii. Electronically recorded interrogations are <u>preferred</u> but not mandated.

iv. There is no statutory or case law mandatory requirement that compels Canadian police to electronically record all interrogations.

v.   Consequently, a trial judge must *justify* exclusion of a non-electronically recorded confession with evidence introduced at the trial. Trial judges are not afforded discretion to exclude non-videotaped confessions automatically and cannot infer involuntariness in the absence of videotape alone.

Editorial: I'm not going to lie – I don't understand this contradiction. It makes no sense to me. A technique that offers a list of positives and no negatives whatsoever is not made mandatory and its absence is not a consequence. This ruling gives the police incredible leeway. They should never complain that interrogation laws are against them.

Volume 1 Conclusion
Ending back to the beginning

The best conclusion for Volume One is the beginning. From the *Oickle* judgement:

"This appeal requires this Court to rule on the common law limits on police interrogation. Specifically, we are asked to decide whether the police improperly induced the respondent's confessions through threats or promises, an atmosphere of oppression, or any other tactics that could raise a reasonable doubt as to the voluntariness of his confessions. <u>I conclude that they did not</u>. The trial judge's determination that the confessions at stake in this appeal were <u>voluntarily given</u> should not have been disturbed on appeal, and accordingly the appeal should be allowed.

*In this case, the police conducted a **proper interrogation**. Their questioning, while <u>persistent</u> and often <u>accusatorial</u>, was <u>never hostile, aggressive, or intimidating</u>. They <u>repeatedly offered the accused food and drink</u>. They <u>allowed him to use the bathroom upon request</u>. Before his first confession and subsequent arrest, <u>they repeatedly told him that he could leave at any time</u>. In this context, the alleged inducements offered by the police do not raise a reasonable doubt as to the confessions' voluntariness. Nor do I find any fault with the role played by the polygraph test in this case. While the police admittedly exaggerated the reliability of such devices, the tactic of inflating the reliability of incriminating evidence is a common, and generally unobjectionable one. Whether standing alone, or in combination with the other mild inducements used in this appeal, it does not render the confessions involuntary.*

Translation:

i. The *Oickle* interrogation started off by consent – only mere suspicion existed.

ii. The suspect was not under arrest – he wasn't in custody.

iii. The suspect knew he could leave at any time because the police told him this repeatedly. The police were honest and upfront.

iv. The police balanced the interrogation – persistence and accusatorial without hostility, aggression, or intimidation. **The most important KEY POINT of the Oickle judgment** – <u>persistence and accusatorial interrogation is not aggressive, intimidating or hostile</u>.

v. The police treated the suspect humanely and civilly.

vi. This was a model "proper interrogation."

End of Volume One but not the end of the book series. Volume Two explains post-Oickle case law.

More Books by Gino Arcaro

If you've enjoyed Gino's writing style, you might want to purchase one of his non-fiction books listed below. Gino's varied careers have given him much insight into business which he shares in his *Soul of an Entrepreneur* series. His *SWAT Football* (technical) series are the result of honing his systems over 40+ seasons of coaching. For a light read, *4th and Hell* is a football story that will sure to entertain as well as inspire. Arcaro's *Be Fit Don't Quit* captivates the imagination of the young (4-8) audience while delivering the message that being active is a good thing!

Comments about any of Gino Arcaro's books are welcome.
Please send us a message through his website: **www.ginoarcaro.com**

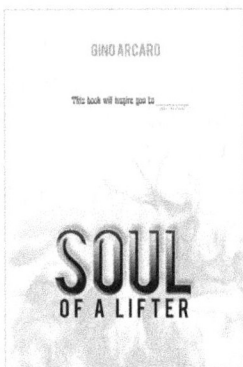

SOUL OF A LIFTER
Gino Arcaro's journey from childhood obesity to natural health and strength was not made alone; he relied on the Soul of a Lifter. In telling this tale, Arcaro draws on life lessons learned from his careers as a football coach, police officer and college teacher to inspire and lead the reader in a soul-searching quest to reach his/her own potential. This is not your run-of-the-mill motivational book. Discover insights about what drives the soul… what happens when you listen and when you don't!

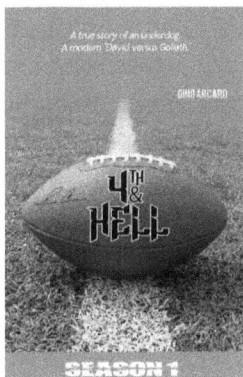

4TH & HELL SEASON 1
"We were David with a Canadian passport, failing miserably at winning just one football game against stars-and-stripes-draped Goliaths." It came down to fourth and hell – a face-to-face showdown. No disguises, no masks, no secret weapons. No one huddled on the sideline. No one huddled on the field. Both sides knew what to expect. No surprises, no guess-work, no mind games. Making the call was a formality. All that mattered was running the play to see what would pass. Someone would execute; someone would be executed.

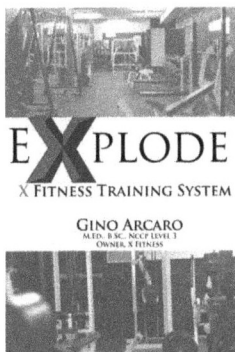

EXPLODE: X FITNESS TRAINING SYSTEM
Sought after his entire adult life to help others achieve their workout goals, Arcaro put his weight lifting theories and routines into this manual. His "Case Studies," true stories from his 40+ years of working out (completely natural) bring a sense of reality to the average gym-goer who just wants to get in shape, stay in shape, and most-importantly, not quit. No gimmicks, just discussion and formulas that can be tailored to any situation regardless of how long or how intensely one has been working out.

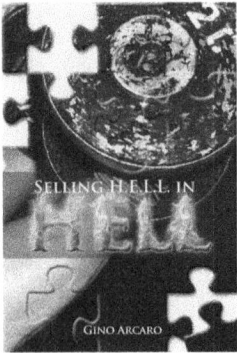

Selling H.E.L.L. in Hell
from the series Soul of an Entrepreneur

You may be starting out in business or just contemplating making the big decision. Gino Arcaro knows what you're thinking and wants to make sure you know what you're not thinking. His thought-bending tales, while entertaining and steeped in reality, will make the would-be business owner take a second and third look at the situation before jumping in. And, for those already "self-employed," Arcaro offers a unique slant on dealing with day-to-day customer and employee challenges.

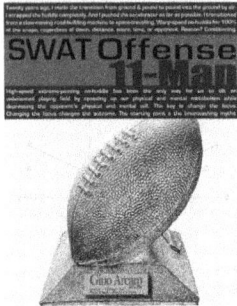

SWAT Offense

By connecting partial concepts that can build any formation, any pass play and any running play to fit the situation, at the line of scrimmage, Arcaro has designed a system that eliminates the need for a conventional playbook that has to be memorized. Memorization is replaced by translation of a simple language. He designed the SWAT offense as a solution to a nightmarish reality of limitations – poor talent and poor resources, a one-man coaching staff, open-admission players, and on top of it all, out-matched opponents willingly sought out! David constantly calling out Goliath. Arcaro's SWAT offense is the most unique offensive system you'll ever see because it has limitless offense capacity but no playbook. A unique feature of the SWAT Offense is its ties to SWAT Defense.

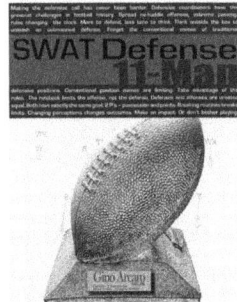

SWAT Defense

Making the defensive call has never been harder. Coordinators have the greatest challenges in football history. Spread no-huddle offenses, extreme passing, clock-changing rules. More to defend, less time to think. Arcaro's SWAT Defense shows how to beat the spread by forcing the offense to go deep and crack under pressure. "A stress-filled workplace for quarterbacks and receivers leads to an explosion." Central to Arcaro's system is his decision-making model that teaches defensive coordinators and players to make the right calls – those split-second decisions that have to be made about 60 times per game. Making the right call is not easy. Like any skill, defensive decision-makers need guidelines and experience to develop into full potential. A unique feature of the SWAT Defense is its ties to Arcaro's SWAT Offense.

Be Fit Don't Quit

Full of exercise ideas young children can try on their own or with a parent, this book will rekindle in any adult a love for the simple act of playing. Gino Arcaro has spent his life working out and teaching young adults about the importance of "being fit." He wrote Be Fit Don't Quit to express a tried-and-true message: Exercising is natural and fun. Never quit!

For more free book previews or to purchase Gino's books go to
WWW.GINOARCARO.COM